The Art of Arranging

The Art of Arranging

Paul Weinman
Joseph Verrilli
Harry Calhoun

Curated and Edited by Leah Angstman

Alternating Current Press
Boulder, Colorado

The Art of Arranging
Paul Weinman, Joseph Verrilli, Harry Calhoun
©1993–2014, 2020 Alternating Current

All pieces in *The Art of Arranging* are the property of their respective creators and may not be used or reprinted in any manner without express permission from the authors' families or the publisher, except for the quotation of short passages used inside of an article, criticism, or review. All rights reserved. Printed in the United States of America. All material in *The Art of Arranging* is printed with permission.

Alternating Current
Boulder, Colorado
alternatingcurrentarts.com

ISBN: 978-1-946580-25-2
First Collected Edition: September 2020

Table of Contents

Just Because I Didn't Leave the Driving to Us I Got Jailed and Juiced Good • Paul Weinman • Reprinted 1993 • 12
    Introduction by the Editor • Leah Angstman • 14
    Bus Tour Ends at County Jail • 16
    Justice—A Matter of Size • 17
    Charybdis • 18
    Melville Made Me Do It • 19
    Open Sez Me • 20
    The Altar Turn I Take • 21
    The Awakened Beast • 22
    Bouncing Off the Canyons' Walls • 23
    Held Stiff Betwixt Knees • 24
    Shipwrecked • 25
    Copped • 26
    The Banana Batch Rag • 27
    Making That Black Pact • 28
    Jail-Side Stuff • 29
    Days of Gravy • 30
    A Loop-De-Loop • 31
    A Shockingly Light Sentence • 32

The History of Candles • Joseph Verrilli • 2003 • 34
    Introduction by the Editor • Leah Angstman • 36
    fall to depths • 37
    the history of candles • 38
    there is something ... • 40
    that cold day • 42
    stillborn • 44
    masochist • 45
    felicia (only once) ... • 46
    saying no to candles • 48
    banshee love • 50
    she has; I have • 52
    a beckoning exoticism • 53
    escaping the scapegoat syndrome • 54

    yes, Mistress, • 56
    the scent of orchids • 58
    the candle's small favor • 60
    lisa doesn't mind • 62
    an ending-of-sorts • 63
    Joseph Verrilli's 2003 Biography • 64
    Acknowledgments • 65
    Author Thanks • 65

Body English • Joseph Verrilli • 2009 • 66
    Notes on the Text • 68
    Acknowledgments • 68
    Author Thanks • 68
    Story • 69
    Portrait of Two Young Women (Certainties) • 72
    One Child in Particular • 74
    The Rhythm of a Saturday • 76
    Tall Tales and Wind Chimes • 78
    Enigmatic Child • 80
    Before the Dance • 82
    The Young Girl as Protagonist • 84
    Innocuous • 87
    Adagio • 88
    Memory as Quicksand • 90
    Malaise: Melancholy • 92
    Woman in Various Stages of Redress • 94
    Pre-Conceived Notion • 96
    Choreography • 98
    Legacy • 100
    A Face Almost Forgotten • 102

Outtakes from Various Publications • Joseph Verrilli • 2003-2014 • 105
    Hearing, Not Hearing • 106
    The Pouring Rain, Even When Undetected • 107
    Sandrine's Lament • 108
    Jehanne's Heart • 110
    when the lack of emotion writes a letter • 111
    Desperado Girl • 112

Look to the French • 114
They Called Her Chimera • 115
Intersections • 116
The Evolution of Fear • 118
Regretfully Yours ... • 120
Going Nowhere Fast • 121
Closer Than Death • 122
Based on the Novel • 123
The Unseen • 124

Near daybreak, with a nod to Frost • Harry Calhoun • 2010 • 126

Introduction by the Editor • Leah Angstman • 130
To my poetic heirs • 131
Echo • 132
Rain, the smile, lightning, thunder • 133
Peach stone • 134
A little death • 135
Stubble • 136
Near daybreak, with a nod to Frost • 137
Ambling between omniscience and obsolescence • 138
That's enough • 139
Straining for profundity • 140
Chasing the squirrels • 141
Work • 142
I forgot to make her happy • 143
Hummingbirds around the hibiscus • 144
Johannesburg • 145
I feel like being a poet today • 146
Health meets the sexual euphemism • 147
Uncle Joe is movin' slow • 148
The oxymoron of small-press fame • 149
Butterfly, here and gone • 150
The promise, 100 percent and what clings • 151
The house, secure, tonight, tomorrow • 152
Elsewhere than paradise • 153
Bikini atoll • 154
Surcease, coming • 155
Susan Alexander, the snow, 1981 • 156
Dog star, protector • 157

          Just before the sound of one hand slapping • 158
          If I had a gun • 159
          Jack o'Lantern • 160
          The last touch of my father's hand • 161
          The poetry game • 162
          Acknowledgments • 163
          Dedication • 163
Retro • Harry Calhoun • 2012 • 164
          Introduction by the Author • 166
          Acknowledgments • 166
          May 22 • 167
          Retro • 168
          Watering Hole • 170
          Wing • 172
          Baseball in October • 174
          Pleasant Valley Before a Storm • 175
          Evening Rainstorm Over Still-Life in Attic • 176
          In the Hallway Outside the Dean's Office at the College of
              Fine Arts • 177
          One for Hart Crane • 178
          Flying Dutchman in a Bottle • 180
          Groceries • 182
          Allegory: The Old Minstrel and Passion • 183
          Courage • 184
          Railroad Werewolf • 186
          Poetry as a Dying Medium • 189
          This Light, That Portraiture • 190
          Sleeping Beauty • 192
          Aging • 193
          Zen • 194
          Infection • 196
          One for Hank Williams • 198
          Long Nights of Sleep • 200
          Hand • 203
          For Jennifer • 204
          Waiting for the Newspaper • 206
          Leaving • 207
          Author Photos • 208

Letter from the Editor

If you'd told me back in 1993 that I'd be putting the first chapbook I ever read into an archival collection in 2020, I'd probably have laughed at you and argued that, no, I'd be riding my hoverboard and eating food in tiny capsules. But here we are. It's 2020, and we're fighting Nazis again instead of flying around in shuttles. Well. The more things change …

This anthology is the first of the archival chapbook collections in our Violet Ray series, and compiling it was a sentimental walk through the past for me. All of these authors are now gone, but I knew them when they were alive. It's a surreal thing to face—the passage of time, holding on to things that have left you. But I've been at this for a long time, and I've carried with me the hopes and careers of a lot of authors.

One of the missions of Alternating Current Press is to keep alive the pre-digital words of authors from the turn of the new millennium, the post-Beat and avant-garde poets of the 1970s through early 2000s who may have had their heydays before the Internet was a widespread thing. It's very easy to get your work out there now, but back when we began this venture, it was all typewriters, copy machines, handwritten letters, postage stamps, and handselling at open mic nights. Bookstores wouldn't touch zines with a ten-foot pole (nor a ten-foot Russian, so the outdated joke goes), and you couldn't find bookfairs in every major city. Despite all that stood in an author's path to getting noticed, there were some reigning voices of the time, and we are working diligently to preserve them for future readers.

You'll find my individual introductions for each of these authors at the beginnings of their sections, so I'll keep this to the brief overview: It all started with Paul Weinman and Joseph Verrilli. Those two, along with B. Z. Niditch, whom you'll find in future collections, were the first poetry chapbooks we got our hands on and published, just as the nineties zine phase was becoming the aughts blog phase. *Just Because I Didn't Leave the Driving to Us I Got Jailed and Juiced Good* is still one of my favorite (and one of the most iconic) chapbooks of the time. Had this chap not fallen into my lap in 1993, I might be a very different person today. Enjoy the adventure, and stay with us for the series. There's more nostalgia coming your way.

O may I join the choir invisible
Of those immortal dead who live again
In minds made better by their presence. ...
—George Eliot, "The Choir Invisible"

Just Because I Didn't Leave The
Driving to Us I Got Jailed
And Juiced Good

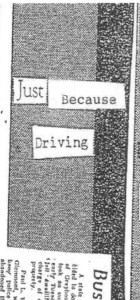

Bus Tour Ends at County Jail

A state employe, who apparently detailed to do the driving himself with one of Greyhound's $85,000 buses, allegedly took an unscheduled run around Albany early Tuesday and is, in Albany County jail awaiting a hearing Friday on a charge of criminal possession of stolen property.

Paul L. Weinman, 31, of Master Road, Glenmont, was taken into custody by Albany police shortly after he allegedly abandoned the bus near the Lake House in Washington Park.

He listed his occupation as a supervisor in the State Education Department.

THE INDIDENT BEGAN ...

The cab driver, believing the bus driver had lost his way, followed and attempted to steer him straight. The bus, he said, while making a turn into Lake Avenue, struck several parked cars, and continued on into the park.

The cab driver said he passed the bus and attempted to stop it, but the driver waved him on before the bus stopped near the lake house and at least two people got out of the vehicle and ran.

HE HAD SUMMONED police over the cab phone and described the driver of the bus as having long hair and a mustache. Weinman, who has long hair and a mustache, was picked up a short time later.

Paul Weinman

Just Because I Didn't Leave the Driving to Us I Got Jailed and Juiced Good

Paul Weinman

PAUL WEINMAN

Introduction by the Editor

Back in the early 1990s, when I started this publishing venture as a preteen, *Just Because I Didn't Leave the Driving to Us I Got Jailed and Juiced Good*—a slim chapbook by Paul Weinman about his jaunty thievery of a Greyhound bus—was one of the first pieces of literature that fell into my lap. First published by Suburban Wilderness Press out of Duluth, Minnesota, then published with funding from a National Endowment for the Arts grant by Something for Nothing out of Massillon, Ohio, then republished yet again by ATH Press out of Pittsburgh, the chapbook had been printed and reprinted multiple times by the time it got to me, undated and with several generations of Xeroxing under its belt. It was a life-altering moment for me. I'd never read anything like this chapbook before—humorous, ballsy, brash, honest, violent, satirical—and it paved the way for Alternating Current Press to publish chapbooks. I first acquired permission from ATH to distribute and recopy their copy of a copy of a copy, and later, a few years before Paul Weinman passed away, he was tickled pink to give his permission for the chapbook to be resurrected and reprinted by us in perpetuity. It's such a good'n—it deserves to keep living on in infamy.

Poet, teacher, and iconoclast Paul Weinman passed away on July 11, 2015, at the age of seventy-five, after a five-year struggle with Alzheimer's. He was an Albany original staple since 1940, often seen riding a curbside-rescue blue girl's bike with a wicker basket in front and an American flag on back, or at urban poetry readings and punk clubs from the 1960s through 1990s, wearing black jeans, black leather jacket, white Chuck Taylors, and geometric earrings, or sometimes nothing at all—he'd show up at local club QE2 completely naked, wearing only a baseball catcher's mask, to read his "White Boy" poems. His poetry was heavily influenced by Beat poets and the natural world. He was an avid camper, hiker, and archaeologist; and taught for forty years at the New York State Museum with his deep knowledge of natural history, archaeology, animals, Native Americans, the Dutch Colonial period, and baseball.

Always a hellraiser, free spirit, and anti-war protestor, Weinman brought his draft card to a military recruiting station in the 1960s, squirted it with a ketchup packet, and ate the card in front of an Army officer. In 1971, he was involved in the incident that would skyrocket him to poetic fame, when he stole a Greyhound bus and took it for a drunken joyride around Albany, crashing into several parked cars and ending up stuck in the mud of the Washington Park lake, whereafter he led cops on a foot chase through the park and was slapped with several criminal counts. After this defining incident, he was diagnosed with anti-social disorder, placed in a mental-health institution, and forced to undergo electroshock therapy. He tattooed a lightning bolt on his temple after this experience and would forever tell people who asked about it that he "must have had a brainstorm."

Here, in all its glory, is his brainstorm.

Paul Weinman with one of his miniature chairs that he made, June 2005.

Bus Tour Ends at County Jail

A state employee, who apparently decided to do the driving himself with one of Greyhound's $55,000 buses, allegedly took an unscheduled run around Albany early Tuesday and is in Albany County Jail awaiting a hearing Friday on a charge of criminal possession of stolen property.

Paul L. Weinman, 31, of Mosher Road, Glenmont, was taken into custody by Albany police shortly after he allegedly abandoned the bus near the Lake House in Washington Park.

He listed his occupation as a supervisor in the State Education Department.

THE INCIDENT BEGAN about 4:30 a.m., when a cab driver driving over Quail Street noticed the Greyhound, traveling north on Quail, make a right turn into Elberon Place—not a franchised route for a Greyhound.

The cab driver, believing the bus driver had lost his way, followed and attempted to steer him straight. The bus, he said, while making a turn into Lake Avenue, struck several parked cars and continued on into the park.

The cab driver said he passed the bus and attempted to stop it, but the driver waved him on before the bus stopped near the lake house and at least two people got out of the vehicle and ran.

HE HAD SUMMONED police over the cab phone and described the driver of the bus as having long hair and a mustache. Weinman, who has long hair and a mustache, was picked up a short time later in the park, police said.

The bus was taken from behind the Greyhound terminal at 350 Broadway, between 3:45 and 4:10 a.m., bus officials said.

This undated and unattributed newspaper clipping from a 1971 Albany paper was pasted to the front of the original chapbook.

Justice — A Matter of Size

The judge glances
across his wide desk
in burled maple on high.
Do you own a car?
he asks with ease.
I say kind of.
And he continues with
What kind of?
A Toyota I say
What color?
Between the rust — blue.
Do you mean to tell
this court, Mister Weinman
that even with eyes
as road-mapped as yours
you can't distinguish
driving a blue Toyota
from a Greyhound bus?
Noise. After the court
is silenced, I respond
It is the wagon model, sir.
Then with a vigorous
wrist flick and a month
in the can, I'm dismissed
till my subsequent hearing.

Paul Weinman

A crusty little cop
long dead to the street
pinches me by the elbow
to take me back to the pit.
But we have to pass
the dozen or so guys
straining to restrain
from strangling, stomping
me on the spot. You fuck!
They'd been arrested, you see
for what I did and considered
me to be a big piece of shit.
But the judge raps his wood
The rest of you — dismissed!
And you can bet your ass
that door wasn't locked
fast enough behind to keep
mine from getting grassed.
Thank me for a night
out of the alley! I yell
as the cell door goes clank
and I get up from the cement
my hand in hold to wipe
some bum's barfed hotdog
across the sweat-wet face
of that creepy cop
his bloated lips in sneer.
First degree grand larceny
how much for that? I ask.
Seven and a half to thirty.
Dollars, I'll take it
hours, you can shove it.

JUST BECAUSE I DIDN'T LEAVE THE DRIVING TO US I GOT JAILED AND JUICED GOOD

Melville Made Me Do It

Melville made me do it
him with his great white whale
and what could I do with no Queequeg
much less an Ahab and only a river
with sick fish and tires too tired to float.
Sure, I ate my draft card, threw stones
at tanks and tore the stripes from the PO.
Yes, I fought hardhats hard-fisted
no Viet Nam for me and marches
black on white to Washington with hair
to my poke, Woodstock rock and weed for smoke.
Still, there was no mysterious leviathan
no behemoth to be my meaning for this life.
Until, be it from behind a Metaxa mind
I saw my Moby Dick ... my trophy in swell
Yes ... a Greyhound bus!
Oh, it was only one of a fleet
parked behind its station in wait
for some journey to New Jersey, Florida
or somewhere to the acid-land of San Fran.
But it was brand new and Scenicruiser blue
striped with chrome, capped in VistaVision seats.
I stopped still that night, yes I'd spied my prey.
That bus would be mine, I swore
my plan ... well-laid.

Open Sez Me

The bars have legally closed
and all my buddies long gone
to beered sleep or broad's teat.
Me, I have 2 shots of Metaxa
on my left and right
some black beauty speed
running off with my night.
It's just three o'clock, the cat
is now my young lion in stalk.
The bus is there, depot's bare
but for the bums asleep
in plastic chairs and switch
of pints from hand to pocket
and back to the Men's again.
I walk the shadows and watch
the street for lights ... none.
The run to the bus's side
is short — there's no door handle
or lock. That's released by magic
a mere pull of metallic logo in front.
Of course, with those immortal words
of Popeye the Sailorman —
Open Sez Me!

The Altar Turn I Take

Mounting the steps
I hold my head high
back stiff with pride.
Each rise of height
brings me closer
to that leather throne
that seat of power
under which all wait
to pay their dues
for individual trips
to separate destinies.
Behind me spirits sit
with confidence, secure
that all the driving
has been left to us
from shore to shore
step to stern
dominus nobiscum
et tu nous
achoo.

PAUL WEINMAN

The Awakened Beast

Well, there I was
a full panel of dials, buttons
triggers and switches to flick.
Knobs for sure and I don't know
my ass from a hole in the ground.
First, the door — pull the lever
shut. Not bad for a beginner.
Now, the engine — no key.
So, I push this and pull that
the lights go on, the horn goes off.
My seat turns right, wipers swipe
and with a low-sounding gurgle
the engine starts up ... up! ...
and away I pull from the station
a smooth sweep of metal and motor.
One man pressing against a post
waves his pint and I flick my lights
throw head back and scream — America!
I've got you in my grasp!
Give me your wretched
Give me your poor
Give me another
shot of liquor!

Bouncing Off the Canyons' Walls

Like the judge later suggested
I should have known the difference
between a Toyota and a Greyhound.
One's got no balls, the other a tail
and certainly there is a bigger gap
between things from one
than in that of the other.
And I will admit
it took a car's side or two
or three or more
for me to judge the distance
between me and thee — sorry.

PAUL WEINMAN

Held Stiff Betwixt Knees

Riding this beast hard
and fast now. Its speed
just the thrust of my foot.
Strong roar of easy power
and silken turn of wheel
an ebony circle that guides
my quick sway around corners
the controlled roll side to side
of streets speedily graced
with the slick sides of my animal.
I turn the knob of distant dreams
signs for Dallas, Boston, Cleveland
and all points west. Then back
to Albany where mythic America
is being made — its wild horses
held in hand — ridden rough
on one-way streets, unfettered
and free and I'm going to cross
the lake so eloquently constructed
in Washington Park — so Victorian.
Sail like the founders of our land
in quest of freedom, riches, pride.
And there it spreads ... placid
moon-sparkled gold! Roar on!
Rage on, oh beast of beauty!
Now ... swim ... NOW

Shipwrecked

Once the wipers got wiping
I thought I'd see fish, old turtles
swimming languidly by — perhaps
some exotics of the Caribbean sort
but no, my bus was stuck, mired.
The wheels only spun, window
showing no deeper than lake's top
and in my wide-eyed stare — muddy.
I tried to jerk forward and back
but no ... the beast just settled
slightly. Opening the door — effort.
And for that, the lake gets let in
almost up to my knees — degrading
end for such a heroic journey.
Looking back over the empty seats
I saw headlights ... crouched quick
and slipped into the water — out.
Heard — Hey, you! Get over there.
Stop! he yelled and I reached shore
ran toward the tennis courts. Stop
or I'll shoot! Now, I thought that's nice
so I started my count of one, two
three, then rolled. And he did the same
except that his bullet did the tumbling
over my somersaulting self and another shot.
I scrambled into the trees, heard car start
and ran furious across the street to hide
in some spirea bush — a beauty siding
someone's last-century mansion—I pissed.
I felt saddened for my blue, chromed beast
wanted a better good morning for it
than being hauled ass-end first
from the dank bottom of that lake.
But there I was, huddled wet and waiting
watching, wondering what kingdom had been lost.

Copped

Between the lace-like leaves and flowers
I watched the early sun spread light
and those police cars in their cruise.
An occasional Paddy-Wagon passed
drunks and punks picked up for being me
probably getting their hocks kicked good.
I waited till just past eight by the bell
when State workers would be strolling by —
me to be just another of your bureaucrats.
Why, I'd ease into that walk to work
and no one would be the wiser, except
for the two fuzz what stopped so fast
I hadn't time to cover my head
from that crack of club and shove
into the backseat floor, hands deftly
clasped in cuffs high behind my back.
Gotcha, don't we Mister Busman?

The Banana Batch Rag

Riding in the Iron Box
was hardly new and certainly
just as hard as before, bouncing
off walls and puke-stiff floor.
Three guys and me cuffed as one
kind of death dance quartet
sharing our lone cigarette.
Unloaded at the County clink
I found undressing was unchanged
anal inspection for saw blades
and lollipops — sure, I farted
in my moon-bend and he remembered
the smell as mine, kicked me clean
across the room. I giggled
and did my jumping monkey dance
hooting, howling sounds of bananas
please give me bananas for breakfast.
Joey, stick this nut in solitary!
Anywhere, I say. Stick me anywhere
but in the nuts with them bananas!
Keep the cuckoo in over the weekend!
You can do anything to me, massas ...
anything — as long as it's bananas
up your asses for breakfast!
And I did my monkey dance some more.

PAUL WEINMAN

Making That Black Pact

Solitary was hardly that —
clank clank of water pipes
hiss of steam, cell doors
opened and shut to see
if I'd hung myself yet.
Hell, they'd all my clothes
said I could have kept
my underpants, but I had none
and there was no bad stuff
to string my young self stiff.
With Monday morn came the nurse
Paul, she said in moan — oh Paul.
Your poor mother — oh Paul.
You see they churched together
so I did my monkey dance
and said I was as crazy as I can
couldn't tell a blue Toyota
from a tomtom — was the devil
that made me do it. OK
she smiled, I understand.

Jail-Side Stuff

Number nine, Weinman
and locked bars behind.
Down the long row of cells
guys seated to the left
sitting, stooping, standing
squatting, smoking, strolling
sprawling, spitting, swearing
sleeping, shitting, sucking
sobbing, speaking, scowling
scratching, seeing, shuffling
scuffing, searching, seducing
seeking, stinking, swigging
swooping, swapping, swiping
seizing, swinging, seething
sweating, sidling, spooning
squeezing, sensing, sending
squabbling, spatting, sinking
shedding, sparring, smoothing
sparing, sneaking, sneering
sliding, shifting, slouching
signing, sighing, siding
shoving, solving, slugging
stroking, singeing, streaking
shirking, stymieing, stunning
subduing, scenting, shocking
and so on with all that stuff.

Paul Weinman

Days of Gravy

Watchainfer?
Copping a bus.
Hey! It's the Greyhound Guy!
Holy shit, that was beautiful!
You shagging us ... you did it?
Some turned quick, smiles popped
others hadn't heard, were told
and shouts went up, God damnits
slapped hard at tabletops, hoots.
A man falls to the linoleum
convulsively giggling as
flowers ease from his mouth
and I start my monkey-jumps.
Some cheer and try to join me
even offer bananas that appear
from nowhere in the thin hands
of a young virgin. And sure
breasts of all hues — some huge
swell from the ceiling. Cell bars
sag and the men braid them closely
into intricate garlands to throw
at my feet — each of the offerings
sprout sweet fruits and old toads.
Turtles, too — many days of gravy.

A Loop-De-Loop

Gotchatho ...
Yes
You mother-fuckin fake!
and ears grow big, flop over
so banana peels can rot.
One dude gets buggered quick
and someone really does forget
whose bed he pissed in.
Cigarettes start running out
faster than they burn deep
into the stripped naked thighs
of probably the youngest inmate.
I begin my monkey-dance
and they all spit, some shit
to throw handfuls of brown
into my jabbering mouth.
I run for my cell
but seven guys are waiting.
They hit me with old tires
cram dead fish up my asshole
until I'm all black and blue
counting blood drops in Solitary.

A Shockingly Light Sentence

Paul, she said. Oh Paul
your poor mother — oh Paul.
You see they churched together
with some lawyers and psycho
shrinks. You'll get out clean
she said what with the time
spent here, a little in there
and some EST thrown in between.
Yes, I say — between my ears.
I saw that nasty movie
with some cuckoo being juiced
to shake anti-social shit
loose so I can be just nice
enough not to shout fuck!
She whispers seven and a half
to thirty I end the sentence
DC I'll take it, AC I won't.
The only Dick I want
is Moby and my own.
So, let the lights go low!
for just a few seconds
or so.

the history of candles

joseph verrilli

The History
of Candles

Joseph Verrilli

Introduction by the Editor

Around the very turn of the new millennium, I stepped outside my circle of known poet friends and began putting together chapbooks by strangers. *The History of Candles* was one of the first I compiled, an endeavor that spanned the end of 2002, came to fruition in 2003, and led me into the reclusive world of Joseph Verrilli.

I knew very little about him, save that he was a hoarder whose letters and boxes always came typed on sheer typewriter paper, smelling musty and old, like they were from a previous century (which, perhaps, they were). When he passed away, his sparse obituary merely said he was 62 and a lifelong resident of Bridgeport, Connecticut, and that he died suddenly in his home on June 6, 2014. All I could ever acquire about the details of his death were that he died naturally and comfortably, and that was the extent of it.

He was prolific with letters, though they were always shy of details, but I remember that he was young when he married his much-older wife, a May/December love that left him alone far too soon when she passed. We once talked at length about how her favorite book had been *A Tree Grows in Brooklyn*, and he wrote of those memories often. What little else I know about Verrilli is that he was a studier of history, often enamored with the idea of (and plagued with the constant dreams of) Joan of Arc and a Medieval past that he felt he, himself, had lived through in another life, another self. At times, this feeling and these dreams bordered on obsession. You'll find several of his Joan of Arc poems in the Outtakes section—some published, some of them never before seen.

The final obsession of Verrilli's was reincarnation. He loved music and children, and he believed souls could be reincarnated through both. He heard whispers in songs. He saw the lives of others through the innocence and curiosity of children. Though he never had children of his own (as far as I know), he tried to be a father, mentor, teacher, friend to many other children he encountered.

The rest of his story will have to be told through his own words.

fall to depths

lost in the mind
of another
a willful journey
pulling me down
to darker depths
whirlpool excursion
where I fail much better
each time
discovering dishonor
and deepening disaster
not that this
was the first time
I've heard the wailing call
on just the most perfectly
inaudible
shriek frequency
I would never
want to return
to the former self
put me in chains once more
mother of mystery and mayhem
a willing journey
lost in the mind
of another
(fall to depths)

the history of candles

the casual observer
reluctantly stares through the shrine
in the musty-smelling living room,
where the falling darkness
of late afternoon
reveals dried palms
framing old photographs
like snake-branches,
the blurred light of swaying candle flame
ignoring demon winds of parched bodies
passing in a rush of denied madness.

the pale sister
sees only what she wants to see,
what her tormented eyes
will show her
in the musky silence
of the dying afternoon;
she views the dim pallor
of candlelight
illuminating what lay
beneath the surface
of her bruised soul,
a torrent of rage rising,
legs pushing against current,
a solitary scream
burying the bright of normalcy
in a white-hot flash of recognition.

the secret queen
puckers her lips into the snarl-smile,
inviting the list that will never be,
tattooing the concrete floor
with the lightning-crack of lithe footsteps.
late afternoon is a memory;
so is his apparent demand
that she sway to his rhythm.
she smiles ... and beguiles ...
and traces the shapes of continents
on his expectant skin
with dripping candle wax,
glistening like religion.

JOSEPH VERRILLI

there is something ...

about the last strains
of daylight
when the overcast sky
sheds foreboding whiteness
over everything
a weird kind of sadness
like guitars
rhythmically strumming
an end-of-acid-trip dirge
as if something is dying
and giving way
to something
completely unexpected.

there is something
about the sloping
of a woman's hips
as she pauses
to smile nervously
in a garishly lit corridor
how her calves
become the contours
of ankles and heels
suspended fashionably
with the worn carpet
quaking beneath her
the sad foreboding
of her reborn wickedness
the way her form merges
with the dark
below the ceiling
and the strange brightness
of fluorescent wall lights
giving the very air
a nightmarish sheen.

there is something
about rebounding tension
that greases the loins
and causes beads of sweat
to form
on creased foreheads
and twitching palms
fear begets anxiety
then comes
the silent wondering
about the meaning of it all
before the sun plunges
like the fall of civilization
when words are tired substitutes
for the something about to explode
like colors like lust
like madness

that cold day

that day that cold day that day of days
the spinster sitting in the park
haggard from death
the slowest kind (in the mind)
surrounded by mist
enshrouding her inert form
halo protecting her world-weary soul
from random intricacies
from the impersonal futility
she grasps like handfuls of air
when gasping for breath
for breath for cold breath for breath of breaths

(breathing)

that day that cold day that day of days
the spinster recalls a dream from long ago
a matter of days or
too many years to have kept track of
she isn't even sure
if the images dancing like pulsing lights
in her haze-ridden mind
could have been banished to dream's landscape
at night when the tension in her body
would have her gyrating with a soiled pillow
the near-dream about the young man
giving her the attention
she didn't remember asking for
first with flowers then with herbal tea
words softer than she had been accustomed to
the dream or near-dream or barely possible dream
turns dark and she doesn't remember anything more
except the sighs coming from her throat the wheezing
the moans the cold moans the moan of moans

(moaning)

that day that cold day that day of days
the spinster sitting in the park
recalling passages from dearly departed books
therese and isabelle was nice
so was *sundays and cybèle*
the fox
clock without hands
the warmth would spread upward
and would seem to have spiraled forever
until she would gyrate (again) into a frenzy
a softer one this time
leaving her more breathless
than she'd ever remembered
her thoughts bring back images from dreams
stubbornly persistent images that refuse to die
the boys on the corner near the café
yellow lights illuminating portions
of elusive haunches
they speak to each other as naturally
as the spinster stealing the lost hope she needs
they laugh and share cigarettes bottles of wine
they share a piss compare the lengths of their cocks
and the laughter continues until they dissolve
into the yellow mist
the mist in the spinster's mind that she curses
the spinster sitting on the park bench that day
that day that cold day that ray of sunlight

JOSEPH VERRILLI

splashes of color
all the sorrow-flecked
tomorrows
the sun tango-dipping
past clouds
dripping whiteness
across the oval dome
of spiritless blue
the witless splendor
down below
abyss of streets
tarmac hills and curves
rising falling erupting
like single-minded paths
of rollercoaster tracks
for bemusement
splashes of color
all the sorrow-flecked
tomorrows
faces glowing at carnival dusk
the violence of love
the humorous sadness
the moon tango-dipping
fingerprints of evil
shadows
on the stillborn sand

masochist

I know I'm wrong
and I know I don't sleep
with common sense
and bring it hot coffee
and bacon and eggs
in the morning
I know I'm not coming to life
on cue
I'm not reading signals
as if a potential smile
depending on it
I'm not exchanging favors
with that everyday casualness
I'm not buttering up the toast
so the first bite
won't taste bitter
and the eating of the rest of it
won't serve a mutual purpose
such as feeling refreshed
or replenished
or doing my part
paying for the breaking
of the fast

I know all that

it must be the pain
that keeps me going
the doing-without
that greases the wheel
and keeps me rolling
through yet another day

JOSEPH VERRILLI

felicia (only once)...

did I hear your voice
in direct communication
with mine
the door was ajar
a sliver of golden light
filtered through
taunting me
for a mere moment
before the door closed
(without a sound)
and the "do not disturb" sign
was draped over the knob
almost
as afterthought

felicia (only once)
did you have anything to say
words
that might have contained
meaning
within their borders
in how you arranged them
a seemingly haphazard
"new world order"
but maybe not
(you aren't saying)

felicia (only once)
did I get to compare you
to historical monuments
in statuesque daydreams
to female icons
from 1930s hollywood
sometimes
all we have
is one fleeting chance
to grasp paradise
but I didn't have
sticky fingers
and you were as slippery
as they come
many have
before returning to mediocre lives
it's almost a cliché
a snicker a laugh a drop in the ocean
a door closing silently
almost
as afterthought

JOSEPH VERRILLI

saying no to candles

perched on my little hill
with my little hands
at my little sides
barely ten years
old
looking down
into the abyss
of incense and candles
in awe of the fear

perched on my little hill
little catholic schoolboy
attending mass
attempting to focus my little powers
on the extravagance before me
my little attention span
so easily distracted
(even then)
by the shock of a certain
facial expression
it was the nun
the first-grade teacher
frightening me
with her green eyes
and ruddy complexion
I almost pissed my pants
(oh dear)

perched on my little hill
inside the catholic church
looking down down down
feeling set apart
from my own contemporaries
staring at the long rows of
candles
in red glass holders
long rows of
candles of dancing flames
of swaying candle flame
frightened by the rigidity
of prayer
my little mind was thinking
about music
its relative freedom
its lack of borders
I didn't want to be there
perched on my little hill
I wanted to be lost in music
no   I don't want this   no
candles can't make me devout
I remove myself from their spell
minds are terrible things to waste
my little shangri-la is beckoning
(where the music is)

Joseph Verrilli

banshee love

they prowl ripped-backside streets
walking tall with the aimless air
of the lusting scavenger
ravaging raptures
with fangs dripping with saliva
and pre-cum
latticework of bloodshot orbs
an anesthetic to the innocently deranged
mascaraed visages appearing surreal
like unwanted images from nightmares
when the day/night brings a close-
up
bizarre reproductions of childhood memories
(best banished and forgotten)
stilted freeze-framed moments
at amusement parks
passing sleazoid facial expressions
of heavenly hustlers at carnivals
bliss
of love
from above
falling like remnants
of a no-frills space shuttle
fluttering like eyelashes
from classrooms of long ago
bliss
of love
making the correct mistakes
in this discordant opera
where the haze of insanity
clarifies itself
through this lens
the split-screen of real-life
the prowl varying in degree
lusterless jewels

The History of Candles

for the fools in ourselves
the banshee behind the counter
in the government building
would have me believing
I am not seeing
what perception translates
as a vision of repugnance
drawn to her face
the layers of makeup
the mascaraed visage looming larger
reproducing itself
(the split-screen of real life)
the concept of approaching death-waltz
a love garden with eyes
walking taller than a cartoon skyscraper
fangs drip-drip-dripping
with readymade body fluids
bloodshot orbs speaking in tongues
the leer of the lascivious
the cooing of mutant banshees
mothers of mayhem
spread-eagled at the bitching hour

she has; I have

Joseph Verrilli

when a woman speaks,
I should listen.
she has; I have.
she offered
what I've been asking for
all along
this unsteady road
of formidable doubt
and cerebral mayhem,
although I wouldn't think
she views it as such,
just the power stance
of someone who is convinced
she is grounded
in these days of outrage,
asserting herself to infinite degrees:
it was verbal humiliation,
at least in tone and volume,
the kind a dominatrix might use
on a sniveling supplicant,
the kind an orchestrator of fantasies
might embellish on audiotape
with the vocal inflections
of the stern schoolteacher.
her public verdict
of my less-than-desirable
character flaws
was meant for me to hear ...
meant to be voiced
in vicious gossip sessions,
forcing me to my knees.
she has; I have.

a beckoning exoticism

hearing beckoning voices
apparently emanating from a close distance
strangely having the decipherable sounds
of the fragrances of flowers
if a sound could jump
into a sense of smell
if such a falsely malodorous ambiguity
were bathed in color
swathed in deepest red
as though it were the sheerest veil
covering dark tresses
protecting a fantasized exoticism
as if one thing could be another
as if a visceral reality
could be queen of falsehoods
a musical sense of illusory embellishment
coiling tantalizing talons
around what is "real"
repeating what would always
translate thought
into something tangible
accessible to touch
with a heart a soul a jump-started mind
hearing echoes of beckoning choices
confusing nearness with distance
siren-calling a mere manchildthing
out of mainstream shadows
fraught with the trappings of darkness
taught the behaviors of the damned
recalling a beckoning exoticism

escaping the scapegoat syndrome

is there happiness
in impersonal slavery
being reminded
of the ancient mysteries
that keep the boat afloat
a dim-witted illumination
you thought had eluded you
or been obliterated
by thought evolving into deception
of the same ground-down self
slipping out messages
in non-recyclable bottles
at low tide—
the low ebb
of the anger
bouncing off the walls
of the racquetball court
back at your face
a halloween prank
hurling eggs on hell night
at the scapegoat
who couldn't find his way to the desert
to be sacrificed
for the mind-frames of the others
smothered
by the frustration
of having mother earth
rubbed all over his face
not even she could
love

is there a begrudging acceptance
of life on the dream-plane
the one left over
when dust seems to have settled
the nightmarish exile
to something grotesque
that hasn't taken complete hold yet
a burgeoning cartoon
flowing from the bargain-basement pen
of the artist gone insane
millennia ago
held in by the walls
the recognizable panels
you learn to love
the sanctuary of the slave
you step outside
accused by varying degrees of languishing
language
of one nursery crime or another
the giggling the patterned intricacies
the timeless rituals the spitball projectiles
not seeing the sunlight
for the clouds raining radioactive dust
forgetting the definition of the word "escape"
learning to love the hatred of circles
a sad distressing comedy
of refused flavors

the sun bursts into view
a matter of moments later
convincing in its all-pervasive brightness
(the self keeps slipping away)

(every body has a role to play)

JOSEPH VERRILLI

yes, Mistress,

inspired by the chapbook
The Red Eyes of the Sky
by Norman J. Olson,
Beaver Lake Press, 1999

my eyes have seen the whores
who have screamed
the coming of the war.
they pretend to have seen quite enough,
but no,
once is never enough
for anything in this slipshod universe
encased between animated borders
that dance the mazurka
of the hopefully insane.
nothing ever happens
until it happens a second time,
the television man said.
but who says anything
anymore?
computer screens glow
like microwave ovens,
digesting fried brains
and miasmic fingers.

your eyes don't see me at play,
running my fingernails
across the blackboard
with an apocalyptic shriek;
your eyes don't pretend to have seen
the deaths of second-shift husbands
in simple rock songs
where keyboard distractions
suggest, hint at,
squint like singed eyebrows
blown along party lines
for no apparent reason.
our eyes don't acknowledge
the courtesies of the damned,
the laughter of the violent,
the tears of the inadequate
who sneeze at sunsets
rather than reinvent salvation
for runaway generations of souls
aborted by fire.

yes, Mistress,
it is your eyes I fear for ...
you might suggest, admonish,
cackle, surrender to terminal ennui ...
even repeat
a recycled penance
the supplicant hasn't the forethought
to have nightmares about;
you cross the street,
hum a simple rock song
as you remember the real things
for a change,
pretend to ignore the whores,
the husbands,
redundant sunsets.
your replacement is being born
in minnesota.

JOSEPH VERRILLI

the scent of orchids

inspired by the poem
"It Was the Orchids"
by Lyn Lifshin

it's that understated, elusive quality
in women
that I'm drawn to,
the part of themselves
not usually shown to men,
almost as if I were lesbian
and they would have nothing to fear
by slouching in chairs in the office
before going home for the day,
shedding skins,
talking about the real things
for a change of pace.
it's that mysterious, intangible quality
in women
that I'm drawn to,
like a moth to flame;
they have known me long enough
to conclude
there is no blackmail on the horizon,
no underhanded bartering
to be forced to endure,
with their having to surrender
innermost corners of themselves
just because it has always been that way.
it's that almost-embittered spark
shining in a woman's eyes
that I'm drawn to,
whose flipside
would seem to be a heart of gold,
an informal impulse
to show me the ropes,
toughen me up a bit more,

offer a few additional insights
on the differences between men and women
and what really makes them women.
there is always the small talk,
a discussion of circumstances
without the usual tension and defensiveness,
a sense of careless abandon
hovering like the scent of orchids,
revealed in all-knowing smiles,
a twinkle in the eye
of the woman casually doing the talking
at such an unobtrusive
and fragrant moment.

Joseph Verrilli

the candle's small favor

none of it really matters, you know.
all the mistakes you've made,
the missed cues, the persistent stupidity,
the glossed-over dreams,
the hollow criticisms,
the emptiness of the conformist values
surrounding you,
the longing for things
you were always convinced
were inaccessible.
the pain has been catalyst
toward your movement even closer
to your particular destination.
just as most people could distinguish
the mark of cain
plainly visible on your forehead
from the other forms
your redundant yearning would take,
now something else altogether
is visible in other places
besides the "furrowed brow."
it's a simple song
about the complexity
of those things age brings.
"something" in this almost-baffling existence
has allowed you
to reach this particular point ...
stronger than before,
despite everything.
the light still burns.
along with the charred remains of burned bridges,
you thought you'd blown out
that one candle
long ago
so you could curse the darkness

in your ongoing love affair with misery.
the flame flickered for a moment,
but wasn't extinguished.
yes, no, maybe ... just words.
there were so many things
you were never able to understand.
candles have personal histories,
just like you.
and neither one of you has died yet.
be invigorated by those small favors.

JOSEPH VERRILLI

lisa doesn't mind

lisa is standing on her front porch.
the orange ball of a sun
bouncing off the borders
of her peripheral vision
isn't part of her mind-landscape,
only an ingredient
to her wandering thoughts
as it sinks
deeper, deeper ...
a star with a mission.
no one knows who lisa is,
or why she stands on her front porch
at this exact moment,
enjoying the coolness
of the slight breeze
as it ruffles her skirt.
but lisa doesn't mind.
she knows who she is,
and where that sunlit revelation
will take her
on a thousand brighter tomorrows;
no, lisa doesn't mind.

an ending-of-sorts

it's over
yet it's only beginning
it depends
on your skin
your eyes
the room without walls
whatever world
you happen to be living in
when your last breakdown was
your last pact
with your VCR
or computer terminal
your last orgasm
your last determined sigh
to end a particular
perfumed dance
in the parking lot
with air-raid sirens going off
like bells ringing
calling you to dinner
whether it's over
or only the beginning
is up to you
however fleeting the image
in your own way of perceiving perception
it can be either

like passing road signs
like traveling
like deciding to live or die
or forget

Joseph Verrilli's 2003 Biography

Joseph Verrilli has been writing prose and poetry since the fall of 1990 and has been widely published in the small press/underground since 1991. Seventeen chapbooks and countless broadsides of his have been in print during that time. He currently self-publishes a controversial poetry/prose/art zine, *Shoes*, and is currently featured on Frank Moore's Love Underground Vision Radio. Upcoming projects include a collaboration with San Francisco poet/writer Maria Kazalia and a future chapbook, *Portraits of a Schoolteacher*. Writing, over the years, has become as integral a part of his existence as breathing. It goes on.

Joseph Verrilli, c. 2009.

Acknowledgments

Some of these poems have previously appeared in: *Lucid Moon, Stardust Memories, Lone Stars Magazine, Iodine, Poetry Motel,* the Marymark Press give-out sheet series, *Liquid Ohio, Sdrm, The Synergist, Cokefishing in Alpha Beat Soup,* the broadside *The Rebels and the Rebellious, Kaleidoscope, Art: Mag,* and *Joey and the Black Boots.*

The Author Wishes to Thank

Leah Angstman, Ralph Haselmann, Jr., Marc de Hay, Milo Rosebud, Jonathan K. Rice, Patrick McKinnon, Amber Goddard, Christa Hart, Suzanne Wigginton, Mark Sonnenfeld, Vermicious Knid, John Berbrich, Bonnie Elizabeth Porter, Dave and Ana Christy, Peter Magliocco, Cari Taplin, and, of course, "Felicia."

A very special thank you to my dear friend Marie Kazalia.

Body English

Joseph Verrilli

Notes on the Text

This odyssey is the third in a series that began with *Portrait of a Schoolteacher*, published by Musclehead Press in 2003, and continued with *Angelica's Story*, published by New Creature Press in 2006.

Body English was originally published in 2007 by New Creature Press before being reprinted by Alternating Current Press in 2009.

Acknowledgments

Some of these poems have previously appeared in *Cokefishing in Alpha Beat Soup*, *Presa*, and *Quarry*.

The Author Wishes to Thank

Leah Angstman, Dave and Ana Christy, Eric Greinke, Roseanne Ritzema, and D. J. Weston.

January 2007

This might not even be true. Sometimes it's hard to tell what's real, and what isn't. Like being alive for a certain amount of years, thinking, "Has all this been a dream?" Or, as a child, staring out the classroom window at a nearby tree on the playground, wondering how long you've let yourself daydream. The boy was staring at the tree as if, perhaps, he were expecting something to happen, or maybe he was just mesmerized by its *stillness*. Was there a breeze blowing, ruffling through the leaves, projecting a certain tranquility? So *life* had been like that for him. Staring, daydreaming, remaining in one position for so long that his sense of time had been altered, or lost; or mistaken for something else altogether.

Decades later he swore he could *hear* the language of his thoughts. "Has all this been a dream?" He'd started out being part of an actual family, going through typical childhood experiences, beginning school, then, at some point, like a bell tolling morosely, he "realized" he was an outsider. Had this happened overnight, was it a gradual process; or had he just been too stupid to see that this had always *been*? Remaining in one position for so long that his sense of time had been altered, or lost; or mistaken for something else altogether.

Being on the periphery of people's lives, whether classmates, neighbors, people in general, became a way of life. It was almost Pavlovian; he felt conditioned to remain "on the outside." Like criticism one hears for so long that one ends up believing it, even though it may not even have been true. Someone tells you you're a loser, ne'er-do-well, good-for-nothing, whatever, and there comes a point you don't even question it anymore. In general, things proceeded that way for years. Acceptance of self doesn't necessarily bring a sense of peace. "You can get used to anything when you have to," as the saying goes. So, existing on the outer rim of people's lives became *familiar*.

This might not even be true. Does hindsight always come with 20/20 vision?

And then he realized he wasn't young anymore. Sometimes past experiences would float back into perception with a certain haziness.

Actual life events seemed so far away, as if they'd taken place a century ago ... the drug/drinking years ... the going-to-rock-concert years ... the years of feeling lost, confused, socially disoriented ... *those* years. Then getting married, something that took him almost completely by surprise; then came the caregiver years. Was all of it true? Or had he been in a cosmic stupor all his life, waiting for clarity to take focus? Did apathy have anything to do with this condition, if it *was* in fact a condition? Within the foggy wasteland of his mind, did 1+1 still equal 2?

The Travis Bickle voiceover from *Taxi Driver* hit him one day, almost like a parody of a parody ... a self-deprecating satire on satire: "And Then There Is Change." He was being led by a force he couldn't see, or understand, moving through places and bodies like some sort of transparent cartoon character, a marionette dancing some strange contortions of head and limb movements that initially seemed to make no sense. Then, The Realization: "Sometimes you have to go backward in order to move forward." Nobody understood this but *him*. Like discovering the politics of learning all over again, like going back to school.

It wasn't *like* going back to school, it *was* going back to school, at the age of forty-eight. Literally, physically, going back to school, as a student, but *not* as a student, all at the same time. Non-events would become actual events.

The reason for going into the second-grade classroom was to volunteer, beginning with reading children's books to the class; then, as time went on, he became an unofficial teacher's aide, in a sense. He remained in that classroom for five years. What was the reason the teacher kept inviting him back, year after year? Had she felt a certain sympathy, because of his feeling displaced by his wife's death a few years earlier? Or was it because she'd liked his reading voice and the fact of his being a help to her in the classroom? Had she been trying to lead him back to some sort of normalized daily life again? Or had it been something else altogether? He could hardly ever figure women out as it was. And maybe the reasons weren't important. One year blended into the next, totaling five.

"One man's ceiling is another man's floor." What is true for some is false for others. Some can see Absolutes, while others seem more preoccupied with those shades of gray. What one person might off-handedly describe as "the unseen force that rules the universe," he recognized as God. Sometime before leaving the school he received the revelation that God had led him there. It was not random, as "secular humanism" might have defined or dismissed it. Now he felt that his life had purpose. The Light at the end of the dark tunnel. Clarity ... at least on days when the sky wasn't overcast, or overrun with the balm of fog.

This story might not even be true. But his heart and mind tell him he was led back into the world of childhood for a reason. Not as a young participant, obviously, but as someone who had gotten lost by the wayside and needed to learn certain things all over again. You can call this a second childhood if you want to. To learn how to live and laugh again, to learn how to be comfortable among people once again, to learn how to pass on some of the knowledge and wisdom inside him to another generation. To learn how to love and trust again.

This might not even be true. You can believe it, or you can choose to dismiss it as too many words thrown together for no discernible reason. But it happened.

JOSEPH VERRILLI

Portrait of Two Young Women (Certainties)

May 2006

She must have been the kind of girl
who would take refuge
in the hazy landscape
of daydreams,
who would feel mysteriously alone
even when surrounded by others,
the classmates she was placed among,
the family she discovered one day
she was a member of.
Even on idyllic Saturday afternoons,
home alone, as fate would have it,
the teenage equivalent
of the same adolescent girl,
feeling comforted by familiar rooms,
yet strangely foreign to them,
would find her silence spreading
like the bright sunlight
filtering through the lace curtains,
an evolving forward motion
without sound
or apparent destination,
studying, with concerted effort,
the dust motes
bobbing and dancing
within the ray of light
coming through the familiar curtains
down to the carpeted floor,
as if this were the most natural activity
to emphasize with her concentration.

In a previous existence
she must have been the kind of girl
who had felt the indescribable beauty
of a distant voice,
like an unavoidable mistral
blowing through her dark tresses,
leading her to a holy destiny,
if surety could be translated,
if the spirit
of one solitary sojourner
could be transferred
to another physical form
centuries later,
the kind of young woman

tugged and pulled by divine currents
to be attuned
to the words within her.

JOSEPH VERRILLI

One Child in Particular

March 2005

There is a certain sacredness
to childhood,
a pure, unspoiled radiance
held in check by itself;
a glow
that will surely pass away,
replaced by life's next phase,
beautifully temporary
despite its own preoccupation
with itself,
its ignorance of Time's
thoughtless death sentence.
Yes, like life itself,
which lasts only a moment,
then extinguished
by its own timespan.
One such precocious child's life
is brought to sharp focus
before me,
as if I were viewing a film
that could be replayed
at any time
within the vaults of memory.
How many little girls
have tried to grow up too fast,
with not one thought
for the brevity of childhood,
how the fickleness of life
would never allow
such an innocent period
to be repeated.
Her name is Melanie,
if one solitary name

could ever be deemed significant.
She has no way of knowing
her life is on display,
that years from now
someone might be reading
these words,
wondering where life led her,
down which unforeseen lane,
and if that very same fickleness
shed rays of kindness
on her unfolding persona.

JOSEPH VERRILLI

The Rhythm of a Saturday

November 2006

That idyllic Saturday
the world felt like a gift
someone had given her.
Barely a teenager,
her existence
felt like a flower
nestled in the palm
of her little hand.
The warmth of sunlight
peeked through the branches
of trees
in a way
she would never forget.
The sidewalks she'd run
up and down
seemed as familiar
as her emotions.
The remainder of the day
would stretch before her
like a song
that would never end.
Her father and mother
reminded her
of a king and his queen
in a timeless fairytale.
Life felt perfect.
News reports from TV and radio
seemed miles away.
She couldn't conceive
of anything
that could erase
the smile from her face.
The blue sky, the sunlight,

the sounds of city traffic,
her carefree dancing
through the remainder of the day
were like paintings she'd seen
in books from the library,
pure, devoid of danger,
as silky smooth
as her long, dark hair
that bounced happily
when she'd walk, run,
dance.

JOSEPH VERRILLI

Tall Tales and Wind Chimes

May 2006

Little Angelica
talking a blue streak
chattering with adrenaline rush
as I walked her
and three others
to and from the school bathrooms
like two friends
who hadn't seen each other
in years

and had lots of chit-chat
to catch up on
I wanted to tell her
to "come up for air"
but didn't want to spoil
this bonus of spontaneity
her relating
that would-be story
of her stepfather sending her
to her grandfather's
convenience store

for cigarettes
and being questioned
by a policeman
who was "conveniently"
right there on the scene
because of her age (eight)
"but it turned out OK"
she concluded
it had been months
since we'd had talks like this

Peace spreads within me
whenever we'd talk
the school environment
merely a backdrop
with the sound
of wind chimes
barely audible
to underscore
the otherworldliness
of these chattering excursions
into conversation

Enigmatic Child

March 2006

Angelica, child of enigma,
daughter of spiritual charisma,
mature for her eight years
in this world.
The tribulation in her child's world
only seems to strengthen
her resolve, and emerging persona.
There have been efforts
to separate our bonding,
our emotional connection
to each other,
which seems as beautifully natural
as the act of breathing.
Sometimes I wonder
at her perceptions of the world
and life so far,
images and impressions
that remain tucked away
in the recesses of her mind.
She continues,
with her unique brand of innocence
and soft, silent boldness
to draw me
into her world of childhood,
as though I were her brother
or father,
or some other member
of her family.
With the Lord's help and guidance
I continue to show deep reverence
for the sacredness of childhood,
a time that lasts
for but a fleeting moment,

something meant to be cherished;
protected.
And continue to show Angelica
the kindness and compassion
she craves,
sometimes without speaking,
garlands of spiritual flowers
for this young lady
who shimmers and shines
like the sun's reflection
on vastness of ocean.

Joseph Verrilli

Before the Dance

for Francoise
January 2007

How the heart dances
to any pleasing or haunting melody
that happens along!
Before the dance begins,
there is that wide-eyed moment
of intangible recognition
that defies mere language:
Epiphany. Satori.
When, in unavoidable disbelief,
later with resigned emotional
convergence,
I first gazed
into your big brown eyes,
heard your heartbroken voice!
Abandoned by your mother and father;
your grandmother
chose to be rid of you.
How could I ever bid you
a final farewell
after seeing, hearing you,
plunging myself willingly
into your story,
the legacy
of a tragic destiny
you did not ask for!

During added verse
to this pleasing, haunting melody,
I grasped
your fear of abandonment
like an errant lover.
Remembering
my own thoughts and emotions
on the subject
at different times
during my own strange, estranged life.
That defenseless innocence
in your eyes,
the resigned sadness
in your voice,
almost philosophical,
that crashes through
and soars beyond
the finite words you employed,
speaking volumes
on the repeated stabbing
of heartbreak, despair.
Implausible, impossible, utterly insane
to ever kiss you goodbye.

Trapped within the confines
of my own broken heart,
I promise to take
these thoughts and emotions with me
to the grave,
where they will be sealed forever.
Francoise wasn't even your real name.

JOSEPH VERRILLI

The Young Girl as Protagonist

January 2007

It was a lifetime ago. Looking back, those days seemed so innocent, compared to the world as it is today. The year was 1973; I was a mere twenty-one years old. At the time, my favorite band was the critically acclaimed English hard rockers Mott the Hoople. Their latest LP, *Mott*, had just been released in England and was reputed to be causing quite a splash. So, of course, being a hardcore fan of theirs, I had to buy this record as soon as it was released here, which featured a variety of musical material. The last song on Side Two was the very poetic "I Wish I Was Your Mother," softer-tinged than usual, featuring acoustic guitars and mandolins, in the general style of the Rod Stewart mega-hit "Maggie Mae." If the voice of frontman Ian Hunter had ever "spoken to me" before with poetic lyrics, this particular communication between singer/songwriter and listener seemed even *more* powerful with "I Wish I Was Your Mother."

Little did I realize at the time that the lyrics of that song would remain buried inside me, only to come to mind years later: "I wish I was your mother / I wish I'd been your father / Then I would have seen you / Could have been you / As a child / Played houses with your sisters / Wrestled with all of your brothers / And then, who knows / I might have / Felt a family for a while."

Seven years later, I met my soulmate and future wife, Janet Ochs. Ours was an extremely chatty relationship. We would always talk about all sorts of different things. The part of her life she'd talk about extensively was her childhood. There usually seemed to be a glow about her when she'd bring certain childhood memories to light.

To this day, my favorite picture of her is a sepia-tinted studio portrait. According to her recollection, she was nine years old when this picture was taken, which would've made it either 1942 or 1943. There was the innocent smile, the happy glint in her eyes, the bow in her hair. This picture certainly spoke of a bygone era that could never be repeated. The preteen years, the influence of the world-at-large still at a safe distance, the basic expression of the photographed child, pure, untarnished, surrounded by a certain sacredness.

These days I've occasionally wondered why I've felt inspired, compelled to write about young girls. Whether via poetry or prose, or something I might be reading, "the young girl as protagonist" has always held a certain appeal for me, the idea of presenting the young girls as a bastion of strength, a metaphor for anyone surviving challenging circumstances, the image of someone unsure of herself and what her strengths might be, yet in the end a stalwart heroine, even if all she is surviving is childhood itself.

At some point during our seventeen-year marriage, Janet confessed that her favorite novel of all time was *A Tree Grows in Brooklyn* by Betty Smith. She also admitted she'd read it for the first time when it was initially published during the mid-1940s. Francie Nolan was the name of the young female protagonist. Set during the early twentieth century, this autobiographical coming-of-age story reveals the survival skills, strength of a young girl at a time when circumstances became challenging, difficult, in the midst of urban poverty. This book, which I read after Janet's death in 1999, never resorts to the maudlin or self-pitying it could have had with a less-talented writer; instead the overall tone is an upbeat one, with one of its main themes being the determination to survive and rise above hard times. And yes, Francie *does* survive her personal and family struggles, so much the wiser. What makes this novel as interesting as it is, is Francie's young age, at least in my eyes, to express burgeoning strength.

While Janet was still alive, I used to say that I wished I'd known her as a child. As it was, she was nineteen years older than I was, so that was something that could never have taken place. Sometimes, though, even when one realizes that something is virtually out of the realm of possibility, the heart and mind might long and yearn for it anyway. I'd often wonder what it would've been like if I'd been an elementary-school student the same time as Janet. Six years after her death, I was thrust in the midst of an experience that, in a sense, was in answer to that wish. I met someone named Angelica. This "meeting" had such a significant effect on me that it became the subject of the chapbook *Angelica's Story*, self-published in February 2006.

It wasn't unlike the simplistic plot of a children's book, or the wish right out of childhood that becomes so much a part of one's intrinsic being that it ends up coming true. As documented in the chapbook, I was a volunteer in the classroom in which Angelica was one of the students. True, I never could have known Janet during her own childhood, but in this instance, I was given a close look at the childhood of someone of generally the same mold, if only for a few months ... sensitive, vulnerable, non-aggressive, set apart from her classmates for reasons not imminently clear. It was quite the profound gift to have been given. Everything Janet had imparted about her own childhood seemed like a spiritual backdrop for the classroom interactions with Angelica.

In this general context, what was exemplified was the awe and wonder of the growing process, its inherent innocence and purity. I got to view and observe the classroom life of a young girl before she could become potentially jaded by life, or changed by life circumstances. It was an experience that will never be forgotten, and brings up the rhetorical questions: Could Janet's spirit have been "inside" this little girl? Or could Janet's spirit have led me in her direction?

The idea of the young girl as protagonist keeps manifesting itself right in front of me, as it were. This past summer, for the first time, I got to see the 1962 New Wave French film *Sundays and Cybèle*, as vivid a portrait of a young girl as has ever been captured on film. And fairly recently a friend sent me a copy of the William Thomas Walsh novel *Our Lady of Fatima*. The children in Portugal at the time of World War I who had seen visions of the Blessed Virgin Mary are written about in detail, including their childhood preoccupations in the years before the appearances took place. These are things that keep "appearing" before *me*, which certainly *don't* seem like mere coincidences. Maybe one day soon I will write a novel with "the young girl as protagonist."

Much has been spoken and written about America's "loss of innocence." For me, these events and books concerning young girls translate, in a sense, as a form of "Innocence Regained." There is much to be learned from children. Those of us who assume we know so much don't know that much at all. Or what we *had* known has been lost with the passage of time, but it's never too late for it to be regained.

Innocuous

December 2006

All day is a long time
for nothing to happen.
"Do not disturb"
reads the sign
in the curtained window
of the deserted house.
What's for dessert?
A small round white cake
on an aluminum pie plate
is held
by two small thin hands,
blond bangs
practically covering
her eyebrows,
minarets of smoke
from the thirteen blown-out
birthday candles
curling and rising
up toward the high slanted ceiling.
No fairytale princess,
this little girl alone
playing "let's pretend"
with the dust motes
sparkling and dancing
in shafts of sunlight
piercing the stillness
with something off-handedly
unspoken.
Her voice would crack
on future afternoons
slightly different
from this one.
The real clues
always seem to materialize
between two innocuous
run-on sentences.

JOSEPH VERRILLI

February 2007

Striving for balance
a balancing of the scales
for direction
that runs parallel
to one's dreams
one's linear expectations
what lies between
the lines
between the day-to-day living
and what lights up the mind
secrets clandestine meetings
and the being led
down paths
not always synonymous
with what is expected
what is almost-casually hoped for
between the laughter
and the reflective moments

Lifted by life
to euphoric heights
for some
downgraded to surprising depths
for others
with so-called adulthood
waiting in the wings
seemingly random circumstances
predestined struggles
some banished
to arrested development

A toss of the fickle coin
or a life-plan
mapped out ahead of time
the girl or the woman
the sliding into success
or the skidding down
coarse embankments
to disappointments
to emotional resentments
to hardship, that somber parasite

What lay between the lines
are secrets
tawdry allegories
bad scripts
with life as the unseen force
the descent into darkness
the by-product
of jaded carelessness
what lay between the lines
is the music of change
for both the resilient
and the vulnerable
the strived-for balance
not always feasible
what keeps one in girlhood
or elevates another into adulthood
never clearly stated
promises
sometimes meant to be broken
like lives like dreams like reality

JOSEPH VERRILLI

Memory as Quicksand

for Mrs. Lucille Overby
August 2004

The muted sounds
of a distant orchestra
might have been the backdrop
for sepia-tinted visions of you,
but with the passing
of the quickened hours
the memory remains inadequate.
It wanes, recedes,
dissolves like steamed water.
To do these images justice
would be like yearning
for a version of perfection
that could never materialize,
nor be conjured up
at the snapping of impatient fingers,
visions of you
swathed within a convenient darkness:
my drinking in your familiar outline
might have been underscored
by somber cellos, violas,
could the dusk of happenstance
be translated to mere sound;
your brown hair mingling
with the convenient support systems
of polished oak flooring,
the desk of austere cedar,
your form gliding
through the glaze of semi-darkness
with the ease of familiarity
with free-flowing surroundings ...

Our conversation
may or may not have been,
though the memory of shared words
tugs at casual remembrance.
Your eyes
dispense recognition,
and I trade the usual uneasiness
for the light-heartedness
you always inspire ...
our disparate existences defined,
clearly.
My movements through your classroom
melding with the spark and dazzle
of incendiary encounter
never brought to flame.

Being in your presence again
could have been real,
if the everyday preoccupations
could have been as muted
as the cellos, the violas,
the orchestra.

JOSEPH VERRILLI

Malaise: Melancholy

for Marie Kazalia
September 2003

When the long night is over,
and I half-heartedly ponder
the chaos
that swirls around me
like ocean tides,
barely can recall
the previous day's flirtations
with all the manipulations
and the chameleon stances,
near-dreams
that might have never been,
I think of you ...
and how you've casually welcomed
the retelling of my tawdry secrets,
my need to confess
events and thought-fragments
within the dark of solitude.
You seemed to be listening
with the rapt attentiveness
of someone lost in the reading
of a captivating novel.
Our exchanges always seem to flow
like rivers
untouched by the wilds of nature.

I think of you, and imagine
how you might be handling
your own flirtations ...
I think of you again now,
after the explosiveness
of your own retold secrets
has ebbed with yesterday's turmoil ...
only because sleep brings a blanket
of semi-forgetfulness,
when everything seems renewed
on any new morning.

Now that the long night is over
and I half-heartedly ponder
what you needed to express,
the chaos of tortures in the dark,
the series of shockwaves
brought on by the anarchy
of ongoing moral malaise,
the endless manipulations,
the changeling stances,
I think of you ...
nothing seems to have been resolved,
nothing has changed
after the emotional upheavals,
except for the passage of time,
the long night
giving way to morning.

JOSEPH VERRILLI

Woman in Various Stages of Redress

November 2005

1. Today
   She was occupied
   with talking to another man
   by the building's back door
   their banter
   intentionally unintelligible
   the wistful longing
   barely evident
   in her dark eyes
   when she held the door open
   this blustery autumn afternoon

2. Two weeks ago
   She was pulling
   an overloaded box
   to the same back door
   an activity meant to convey
   it belonged exclusively
   to her woman's world
   but seeing her struggling
   something inside me
   told me to make restitution
   for past infractions
   I picked up the box
   carried it inside
   preoccupied momentarily
   with the way her full lips
   ascetically complemented
   her brown skin

3. Months ago
   The first time I laid eyes
   on her
   in the stuffy laundry room
   the highlight of what I beheld
   were her eyes
   tinted with melancholy
   a disciplined silent longing
   a tragic gaze
   of a recalled restraint
   I decided not to speak
   to her at all
   but couldn't banish
   to forgetfulness
   the way her full lips
   complemented her brown skin
   a saintly countenance
   that should have been captured
   in a stained-glass portrait
   from long ago

JOSEPH VERRILLI

Pre-Conceived Notion

May 2005

I think of you now
after all these years
pondering
the brevity of life
and how much time
I might have left
before it all ends
before the breath
leaves my body
and the rapid decaying
begins in earnest

I think of you now
if you will be hovering
in the vicinity
as I lie in the operating room
unconscious
surrendering to the events
and circumstances
taking shape
without my knowledge
will a part of me
be able
to look away
step outside of myself

I think of you now
wondering what will orchestrate
my future demise
is it your spirit
that will come for me
illustrating
the pre-conceived notion
that nothing could really
ever separate us
that my body and soul
were always
aligned with yours

Joseph Verrilli

February 2007

Intersecting lives
as diverse
as cultural differences
as the intricacy
of the cosmic latticework
of the unexpected
that bear more in common
than can be perceived
by the naked eye

Intersecting movements
as predestined
as they are spontaneous
as true to form
as the ballet
of life experiences
set to music
both abstract
and clearly expressed
in the visceral language
of life-phases
repeated
captured on canvas
over the passing centuries

Intersecting struggles
as painful
as they are liberating
as cathartic
as gold cast into the furnace
molded by unseen hands
and transformed
by form and process
into something
that hadn't existed before
as natural
as a forward motion
decided upon
after the peripheral chaos
after countless confrontations
with confusion with imperfection

Intersecting sufferings
that translate
as the choreography
of one physical form
replacing another
one life evaporating in the mist
and another coming into being
intersecting life histories
that bear more in common
than could ever be perceived
by the naked eye
than could ever be explained away
in the simplicity and complexity

of a passing heartbeat

JOSEPH VERRILLI

December 2006

Beauty,
elusive Valkyrie,
unpossessable,
not meant to be tarnished,
its mysterious fragility
and personal history
not destined for casual ownership
or for the vagaries
of a filthy, imperfect world,
a translucent holiness
hovering in the eyes,
the angelic voice
as timeless
as abstract music
intoning such lofty ideals.

Beauty,
elusive Valkyrie,
when defiled
by the possessive talons
of demons, satyrs, vile men,
cursed
by their violent intentions,
their intrinsic lack of vision,
emerges
from the tumult of darkness,
from unutterable catastrophe
as martyred Spirit,
the holiness in the eyes
now melancholy, pious,
like that of stained-glass figures
gazing longingly upward,
the timeless music
of the angelic voice
now a tearful fugue
played with hushed splendor
on a majestic pipe organ,
like pearls cast before swine
trampled, rent to pieces,
then resurrected
to a celestial zone,
Purity's sanctuary,
Beauty vindicated,
far from the machinations
of spiritual rape.
Intone a lofty-hearted dirge
for slain Beauty,
reborn Valkyrie.

JOSEPH VERRILLI

A Face Almost Forgotten

August 2006

Closing my eyes
for a mere eternity of minutes
early one morning
cherishing the beauty
of silence
before the world
would roar to life
with its usual amalgam
of city sounds
I catch a glimpse
an elusive illumination
of a forgotten
female face
someone from the past
someone who had glowed
almost as though she had existed
between the lines
between the sublime spaces
of the lives and influence
of more concrete
individuals
a face embroidered
with a holy innocence
with a warm guileless smile
that could melt
the most hardened of hearts
but just as soon
as her face had materialized
in my mind
it was gone
an evaporated vision

I can only wish
her beauteous face
her calming visage
will come again
will come again
and stay much longer
the next time

Outtakes

Joseph Verrilli

JOSEPH VERRILLI

Hearing, Not Hearing

The three veiled, robed figures
walked slowly, without speaking,
as if part of a funeral procession,
down the long, stone courtyard
adjacent to the cathedral.
All three were women.
The oldest, flanked on either side
by her companions,
bewailed a soliloquy
about her lost daughter,
not a young victim of aimlessness
or of the world's wickedness,
but still lost to her forever,
burned at the stake
for being a model of sanctity
that few recognized,
or dared accept.
No one but the old woman
could hear the heavenly choir
spiraling with operatic splendor.
The execution
was now just a memory,
but such a vividly haunting one.
No one witnessing
the young girl's trial by fire
heard the angelic voices
rising up past the smoke
with melodic abstraction,
only the girl whose life
was ending,
just as, years earlier,
no one could hear, discern
the same heavenly voices
that set the girl's mission
in motion,
that ended with her execution,
save this anointed young girl.

The Pouring Rain, Even When Undetected

Nobody leaves their place in line,
or steps outside themselves;
like a play rehearsal,
or figures captured permanently
on celluloid,
everybody remains true
to their assigned roles.
Such a stance
may not necessarily
speak of dignity
or struggle-sculpted character,
but it would seem
part of the cosmic script.
Agendas need full-body massages,
egos need stroking
like various wood-shapes
in a rebuilt fireplace.
Perhaps no one has considered
an alternative scenario,
or maybe things
are supposed to be this way.
In dreams
I manufacture an image
of a disheveled ne'er-do-well
doing more than running
through a torrential rainstorm.
He shouts "No!" to the order
of societal inertia
before either being hit by a car,
strong-armed by the police
or thrown into a padded cell.
To feel the balm of spring,
to see cities and towns
slowly coming to life
each morning,
no one would think
anything was wrong;
or out of place.

JOSEPH VERRILLI

Sandrine's Lament

Oh, how the mighty have fallen!
Sandrine would think those words,
other times utter them,
the way someone
might attach themselves
to an exclamation
that almost became second nature.
This was in reference to herself,
meant as lighthearted paradox:
because she left her mother's house,
needing the protective covering
of individuality,
because she hadn't remained true
to her station,
older women would sometimes
beseech her with whispers
to proceed with caution.
It was the fifteenth century,
after all.
"Look at what has befallen
the Maid,"
they would remind her.
She was burned alive
for heresy, apostacy, sorcery.
Such were the times.
When anyone didn't conform
to what the Church thought proper,
when behavior
seemed even superficially unacceptable,
there was always the possibility
of being condemned, put to death.

"I'm no sorceress,"
Sandrine would exclaim.
"I just want to live on my own terms."
She didn't chase after soldiers
like the prostitutes did,
neither did she espouse revolution;
but circumstances did not bode well
for her,
having left home and lived with a man,
forced to raise her daughter
on her own,
living in a section of the city
frowned upon as morally questionable,
working at an inn.
At times she'd been forced
to send her daughter
to stay with her mother.
"Oh, how the mighty have fallen,"
Sandrine would lament,
tolerating the gossiping townsfolk,
but holding her head up high,
now living alone,
the man imprisoned
for crimes of immorality,
now attempting to rebuild
a tumultuous life,
this Sandrine, this solitary sojourner
in times that she felt exclusively
foreign to.
Deep within herself,
it *was* a lament.
She was only human.

Joseph Verrilli

Jehanne's Heart

And they burned her at the stake,
she who signed her name "Jehanne,"
commonly known as the Maid,
for "crimes" fostered
by the superstitions
of the Middle Ages,
out of fear, hatred, jealousy,
she, formerly shepherdess, farm girl,
who declared
France would have no succor
save by her, and her alone,
pious young French girl
criticized and ridiculed
for praying too much,
virgin warrior,
daughter of God,
patriot extraordinaire,
whose greatest victory
was returning her countrymen
a long-dormant sense of hope,
whose sympathy and compassion
overshadowed her death,
whose last words
were the repeating
of the name of Jesus,
of whom it has been said
that her heart was not consumed
in the fire
but remained whole, full of blood,
posthumously honored
as the Heart of France.

when the lack of emotion writes a letter

the real message
waits between the lines
like a marauding dimwit.
lying in wait for the best opportunity
to pounce on baseless victim.
or did I mean faceless?
no, faceless could never inspire
such venom.
SORRY.
I promised I wouldn't
give in to emotional demands.
I vowed to this pad of paper
I wouldn't surrender my mind.
I wouldn't trade in
the logistics of logic
for a wayward heart.
never mind what that means.
let's keep it simple =
there's already been another remake of
Invasion of the Body Snatchers and
I'm just a pea in a pod
trying to say the right things,
keeping MUM about the rest,
affixing a HALF-smile to this ingenuous face,
pissing my pants and blaming it on
getting old.
I'll die soon. [so there.]

JOSEPH VERRILLI

Desperado Girl

for Pat Steele

The word "desperate" doesn't apply,
but right before my very eyes
the letters rearrange themselves.
"Desperado."
Hi-tech times, strange weather patterns,
interpolated behaviors
of surrealist politicians
and indifferent barristers
bring out a side in her
nobody knew existed.
"Girl."
Society refers to women as girls,
despite their ages,
loss of innocence,
an evaporating grasp
on an ordinary everyday life.
She becomes Desperado Girl,
an irreversible condition,
like certain diseases.
Jailed, shackled, condescended to,
shuffled off to courtrooms,
increasing sleepless nights,
the many disappearances
of former practices, preoccupations.
(Where is the light in her living room?)
She could very well become
the post-modernist Bonnie Parker,
but instead of robbing banks
she could commit random crimes
chosen like door prizes
at a bingo bonanza.
Desperado Girl
is capable of anything.

Like the scene from *Thelma and Louise*
when Susan and Geena realize
there is no turning back.
Even the improbable is possible,
dormant desires for justice
spiraling to the surface
as a vortex of flames
that brings sobering recriminations
from the fools, the rogues,
those who had written her off
as anything but
Desperado Girl.
More has been lost
than mere innocence.

JOSEPH VERRILLI

Look to the French

Where have you gone,
they ask of the Revolution.
Were you merely a mistral
dissipating in dry summer heat,
a mistress of malcontent
cast aside
for the call of compromise
and corruption
knocking at the door,
bearing a bouquet of wild orchids?
Or are you orchestrating
your own resurrection
in underground chambers?
America's ruling class
continues to oppress and exploit
the poor, the disenfranchised,
the working class:
the Bolshevik ethic
making a ghostly resurgence.
Look to the French,
to Baudelaire, Voltaire,
to Camus and Robbe-Grillet,
look to the French Revolution,
when the guillotine
worked overtime;
look to Joan the Maid,
sorrowful over injustice
for so long
until she stolidly grasped her banner
and embraced the mantle
of Holy War.
As the man once said,
it will not be televised.

They Called Her Chimera

The names and insults
were almost endless,
the derogatory sentiments,
the curses and worthless
aberrations of speech
in differing languages, dialects:
witch, magician, sorceress,
devil's messenger,
child of confusion,
diviner of evil spirits,
insane, deluded soul; chimera.
And yet it is always the one
with extraordinary gifts,
with a God-given mission,
with the shield of holiness
who must endure the abuses,
the ignorant machinations,
the resultant persecution
before deliverance can come.
"All the day long
we are counted as sheep
for the slaughter."
And, more often than not,
the deliverance,
the ultimate victory,
is death.

JOSEPH VERRILLI

Intersections

The liquid texture of flowing thought
colors the emotions
with myriad hybrid hues,
like waves of a royal-blue ocean
lapping against a weatherbeaten schooner
that has set sail
for parts unknown.
Nothing in the world
would seem to be completely pure
or flagrantly original.
Through the unending succession
of passing centuries
the initial colors
became shadows of their former selves;
the most captivating emotions
are melancholy, misty-eyed happiness,
the most difficult to deconstruct,
almost impossible to transcribe
or translate.
Like attempting to decipher
if the formations of letters-cum-words
on ancient parchment
are authentic.
Staccato rhythms of enjoined cellos
underscore the very nature
of this liquid texture
flowing like the deepest blue ocean.
Journeys embarked upon
seize the day
like the chorus of an abstract melody.
Reaching for the intangible,
grasping at the unattainable
with a rippling undercurrent
of melancholia, tearful happiness,
flying into the realm

of knowledge and wisdom
with a heart ever beating
with still purpose.
Like that abstract melody,
there are circumstances
that could never be transcribed
or translated
as to be automatically understood.
The emotions have been dabbed
with color,
one thought becomes another,
never to exist in quite the same way
ever again.
But a yellow rose
will always be a yellow rose.

The Evolution of Fear

She is almost brightly named
when queried
if fear is a game
with anarchist rules.
Something alive *can* be created.
Merely a child of her time,
despite her rapidly advancing years,
amid thunderclaps
and crackling lightning strikes
proving
complexity cannot exist
without its simplistic counterpart.
"She plays her part
so he can play his."
She views the prominents
of her time,
is forced to bear their murder
of language,
detests their abhorrent politics.
Every age has malcontents
like her,
silently cropping
the hair of discontent
with jagged shears,
to match the roughness
of her sense of aggression.
The fear of living is much worse
than the fear of dying.
She has cultivated the ability
to stare the philistines
straight in the eye
and cause them to blink, to wince,
to pause,
without doing so herself.
If calamity comes,

anarchy, revolution,
she will find the antidote to fear
and shriek defiant diatribes,
pulling up blind strength
like a viscous membrane.
From whichever partisan view,
she rises, in transcendent victory.
Being uncompromisingly brave
cannot exist
without first knowing fear.

JOSEPH VERRILLI

Regretfully Yours ...

Of all the petty, small-time regrets
that litter my mind
with so much redundancy,
one outshines all the rest:
that I wasn't born French
and living in the early 15th Century,
to have seen Joan of Arc:
not necessarily to have known her,
but just to have seen her,
clad in white armor
riding her horse swiftly,
to have watched her
with her fellow men-at-arms,
to have observed her going to Mass,
to have caught a mere glimpse
of this anointed young girl
who has had such an effect
on me,
my role model,
my patron saint,
my ideal,
and as intangible and inaccessible
as this dream is,
this wish,
this longing for something
that can never be,
but which consumes my mind and heart,
a yearning
that dwarfs all my problems
and petty, small-time regrets.

Going Nowhere Fast

Sleepless dreamless
body weary yet wide awake
mind blazing with leftovers
from this day that day
mouthing wiseass soliloquys
to those
populating my little insignificant
world
the anger the resentment
the utter stupidity
of a life
that has outlived
apparent usefulness
tossing turning
with a laughable vengeance
how much longer
will this charade-of-a-life
be permitted to continue
I'm older I'm tired
longing for sleep
stuck in forced social withdrawal
in forced denial of anything real
I wonder when I'll drop dead
(and from what)
mind just won't shut down
for the night
get up have a smoke
fiddle with the cell phone
throw myself back on the bed
for another round
with sleepless dreamless
the pointless urban
going-nowhere-fast
blues

JOSEPH VERRILLI

Closer Than Death

It's been said the closer
you come to your destination,
the more you veer off course,
riddled with the bullets
of distraction, preoccupation
and the vagaries of self-doubt.
They all resemble a drug
meant to slow you down
and blur your vision.
Your mind might be acutely
aware
of your personal purpose,
but not your heart.
The two need to be melded
together
so that you can return
to your place in line,
your particular spot
on the cosmic treadmill.
And when you are buffeted
by the all-too-familiar
everyday obstacles,
you might become bored, listless,
in dire need
of some great change.
Closer to you than death itself
is all the trash
you must wade through,
like being half-submerged
in a toxic ocean,
pushing your legs forward
against the current,
against the grain,
which feels like
an insurmountable mountain
you tell yourself
you cannot climb.

Based on the Novel

Pain, ignoble circumstances,
being born, unawares,
beneath a blood-red moon
leads some to become cynics.
And what makes someone jaded?
Self-deception?
Inflated notions of one's importance?
Grasping at knowledge
without reaching for wisdom?
Know-it-alls;
we know all about them.
They people the planet
like chronic illness;
Bob Dylan once made mention of
"the disease of conceit."
But why skim through the novel
when one can read it
cover to cover?
The chapter you missed
holds the key
to what you lack.
Books are adventures
that take the reader
on mystical odysseys
with many twists and turns
to a definitive conclusion.
If you haven't read this novel,
your cynicism, jaded sensibility,
your illusory knowledge
are merely
half-baked states of mind.
You need to read the entire novel
with the awe and wonderment
of a child
who has just discovered
the experience of reading.

JOSEPH VERRILLI

The Unseen

Incredulous, she asked him
what he meant by
"the bioplasmic universe."
The older man
waved his arm across the sky
in a sweeping arc
and explained:
an unseen record
of every thought, word, and deed
from the past and present;
the future.
He went on to elucidate
that sometimes
we rationalize what our senses
reveal to us
and that occasionally
a connection is made
between the physical world
and the realm of timelessness,
and have what clairvoyants
refer to as
"a vision."
It's said the dead
speak to us through dreams.
My own experiences
tell me
the dead also arrange events
in our everyday lives
and give us gifts
in the form of random circumstance,
if a connection has been made;
if one believes what is true,
the physical world itself
shrinks in importance
and the unseen

transform us into spiritual beings.
Some say there is no such thing
as coincidence,
that there are no "mistakes"
in this life.

Near daybreak, with a nod to Frost

Harry Calhoun

Near daybreak, with a nod to Frost

Harry Calhoun

Introduction by the Editor

I suppose it's not very nice to start right out by saying that Harry Calhoun was a royal pain in the arse, but, well, anyone who knew him probably just got a chuckle out of that. Calhoun *was* a royal pain in the arse from an editor's viewpoint—always finicky about every word, every comma, never took suggestions, wasn't open to compromise, would spit in the face of style guides, conventions, and editorial commentary. He was a man who knew his words, but rarely knew himself—vacillating between extreme happiness and extreme despair, sometimes within the same hour. He loved his dogs, absolutely adored his wife Trina, and was just beginning to settle into himself and the calmer parts of his later life when his heart simply stopped, quickly and painlessly, on Halloween day, 2015, at the age of 62.

My first major work with Calhoun started when I was back in Boston, with the publication of his chapbook with Alternating Current, *Near daybreak with a nod to Frost*, circa 2010. I'd known him from around the small-press scene for a while; he was one of the staples at the time, formerly an editor of his magazine *Pig in a Poke* and its little brother *Pig in a Pamphlet*, and one of the last remaining poets who'd known and worked with Charles Bukowski and famously battled with Bukowski's publisher, John Martin, who objected to Calhoun publishing Bukowski's work in a standalone edition of *Pig in a Pamphlet*. *Near daybreak* centers around Calhoun's love of his aging dog, Alex (who was later replaced by the two lab-mixes that survived Calhoun: Harriet and Hamlet), nature, and his various wives, with his last wife being *the one*. He loved Trina dearly, and she was the subject of many of his poems; his world seemed to collapse when she was away.

In 2012, I worked on his next Alternating Current project, *Retro*, which was a collection of his older poems from the 1980s and 90s. It is a fantastic slice of his life. A reader can see him grow, come of age, and progress through various stages of love, grief, and self-awareness, and we get an intimate portrait of the young Calhoun, from his brush with death following a stroke to his first few broken hearts from old girlfriends. He was witty and smart, and those traits are intermingled with his humor and compassion. Few things come close to his compassion for animals: "the dog—I love him so much I hesitate to call him mine—," and Calhoun had a vast, unwavering heart for the indie press, for supporting it and ensuring that it grew and grew. Yes, he was a royal pain in the arse. Yes, I knew him like you know a rare leaf. Yes, he was loved and is missed dearly in this corner of the indie press.

Near daybreak, with a nod to Frost

To my poetic heirs

with concept from Kate and Leopold

I'm like a dog seeing a rainbow
without the color sensors.
I know how this works.

I just don't know how to describe
the electricity, the underwiring
that makes it happen,

the botox that makes these old observations
dewrinkle and makes time flow backward.
I can hope that I, a knight-errant graybearded

with three-day stubble, can connect someone
young with something ancient and true,
connect with this old face and older truth,

here is the dog
here is the rainbow
here are my eyes

do with them what you will

HARRY CALHOUN

for Trina

Let me echo you
and you can echo me
the voice carried over the canyon
and bouncing back.

Bouncing joyously like our black Labrador
alive all over the seashore.
Today I walked him and watched him
sensing other worlds than he had known.

He reported back bouncing excitedly
about the joys he had found
and I came back to our door knowing
we had rebounded back to you.

The urge to echo escaped
to the seashore, what could be
more eternal, I glimpsed it
and came home eager to get back

to you
to you

Rain, the smile, lightning, thunder

Action precedes emotion.
But tonight's soft rain
falls before the smile's muscles rise.

Lightning precedes thunder
and who really cares what comes first—
something happy is punching me in the gut

tonight and it feels like bottled lightning,
roars in me like thunder but mellows down
to soft rain on the skylight

that will fill with sun in the morning

Harry Calhoun

Peach stone

Work is that peach stone
sprouted but bearing no fruit
in the pit of my stomach

at three a.m. income is no compensation
as my love sleeps beside me
and the dog—I love him so much

I hesitate to call him mine—
sleeps on his dog bed beside us.
It seems only a matter of time

before I stop confusing the peach stone
with the tree that shades me
and I roll half-asleep

to and fro to either side
of the bed and connect
with the right decision

Near daybreak, with a nod to Frost

Something wakes you in the dark narrowing
into fall approaching winter, the gap
the orbiting earth always forces
at this time of year. Wakes you
half-asleep still slithering against the pillow
and sheets, feeling that the only barrier
between you and this insomnia
is the satin liner on the coffin.

You chose it for your mom, then your dad.
You picked out their resting clothes.
You did what you could, this is
what it is. There is nothing more yet
something wakes you and you write it down.

The pillowcase is inviting, but it is night
close to morning and there is plenty
to think about. A clock ticks, distant,
and in the lovely furnished bedroom
you've crafted you draw a breath and realize
that something in you is happy.

And might as well be, for now.

Stubble

Kissing, you don't want the remnants of beard
to graze your face if I don't shave.
But I don't like to shave every day.

So an eighth-inch of stubble
becomes an issue that grates
on both of us. And the stubble, the grating,

if that were the worst of it, would not
be so bad. There must be a way to start talking,
to come closer than that last irritating

eighth of an inch

Near daybreak, with a nod to Frost

Scenting turpentine, trees blossoming gum
into the numb arm of morning
dark still and damp with tree frogs
and the overcast promise of some vague tomorrow

so soon to come. The dog beckons
eager to hunt but eager too
to stay fast beside you
waiting in a still-warm sleepless night

for the next noise, the next nose
the next word to drop like a moist
breath in a mossy ear
something fragrant and earthy,

close to the forest's edge
where birth first crept into life
and looked into a dark beyond
and paused before entering

the grassy, peaceful tomorrow

Ambling between omniscience and obsolescence

Your dog lopes in the summer fan of yard
angling out from beyond the deck
and the fence is his, and you look up
and the stars inscribe your eyes
with years beyond, light years but all
you can see is the light, good enough.

you call the black dog almost invisible
out there outside back in
to your little pool of light. Sometime soon,
of course, you will not be able to write this.
But tonight with your wife and a few good friends
you shared a good bottle of wine or two

that you trusted to change as slowly, sweetly
as this gentle leisurely transit from life
to ... wine, shall we call it wine,
let's not call it forever of final,
let's call it wine, this aging,
it just keeps getting better

tasting it so far is fine

Near daybreak, with a nod to Frost

Trina is leaving. Business, necessity.
Four nights, five days away.
I understand business and necessity
but my first business and necessity
is having her back safe and with me.

She is faithful and brave
and I don't fear for her
but I am lost until her GPS
finds me and my welcome hug

again

Straining for profundity

This morning
after a minimalist
bowel movement

and a minimum
of poetic inspiration
I wonder why I even

give a shit

Near daybreak, with a nod to Frost

Chasing the squirrels

90 pounds of Labrador glowing
black as an overcast night
and hopping to be let out

I open the back door to the deck
and he bolts like a thoroughbred
from the gate and if squirrels

could not climb trees or if
dogs could fly he would be
Von Richthofen, ace of dogs,

and in my mind he is but maybe
I just empathize, waking most mornings
to words hanging high in the trees

poems like squirrels taunting me
and I stare up but cannot quite
reach them

Work

I slip into e-mail hell still not showered
so far it's OK, but I've got maybe 30 minutes
until some dumbass drags my life
like a dream of the skinned carcass
of my beloved dog across a burning, sandy desert
but this is no dream, and I can't wake up,

only record this moment
and move on and if there is anything
worse than my dog skinned
dead and unfeeling it's being alive
in this skin and feeling
but I guess I'm lucky

at least the dog is a dream

Near daybreak, with a nod to Frost

I forgot to make her happy

Wine has its alcohol,
subsumed at its best in an avalanche
of flavor and nuance and change

and I became and we became
pure alcohol that without the sweet
impurities became tasteless

and toxic and I forgot
my equivalent of the winemaker's craft:
balance, the alcohol more a side effect

of the fermentation, the subtle art
of bringing out the happy glow

in the cheek of the fruit

Hummingbirds around the hibiscus

There are hummingbirds around the hibiscus
blooming on my back deck
and I could watch all day as they
flirt with the blossoms and I have a poem
about Uncle Joe from the old *Petticoat Junction* show
floating around in my head
and my wife just came out of the shower naked
and any and all of these
seem more important than dragging myself
off to do my job, but Uncle Joe is long gone,
my wife is already dressing for work
and the hummingbirds will flit off soon
as the fall struts its cool self in.
The job and its pains and its paycheck
reach from my tiny office
to ruin it all with permanence

or at least security.

Near daybreak, with a nod to Frost

Johannesburg

I read that Johannesburg is the world's largest city
not on a river, lake or ocean. That's what I read.
Water is important. But what I know for sure

is that my grandmother could not drink water
just before she died and I remember feeding her
ice. My mother, well, she died like a vapor

before I could even feed her goodbye.
My father anointed his dry mouth with a swab
dipped in water the night before he passed.

And I wake up and reach for the bottle
on the nightstand and just before
the water passes my lips a thousand thoughts

enter my mind and I drink anyway,
thirsty, but what choice do we have, really,
but to stay close to water

for as long as we can

I feel like being a poet today

Work doesn't creak in the right key
on the loose plank of the hardwood floor
as I step through the doorway from my bedroom.
Office and typing don't cast the same ochre shadows
as writing longhand, the egg-yolk pencil and its lead
etching lines in the sultry bedroom on the yellow pad.

Poetry is such a creative way of saying,
"I just don't feel like getting up today."
I feel like feeling, doing work I don't get paid for,
and the cocoa and brown contrasts
of our new bedroom furniture are to die
to describe. Like pouring chocolate milk

into espresso, adding Venetian-blinded light
and waiting for it to ignite. And I would step outside
this splendor why? I imagine having a swig of brandy, the color
of gasoline that fuels me to the beach, the drowsy alcohol
that lulls me to sleep, where I dream
that I have to work to keep on creaking

in whatever minor key
these old bones move to

Near daybreak, with a nod to Frost

Health meets the sexual euphemism

In the crisper drawer
sodium-laden lunchmeat
I must hide the salami
from myself

Uncle Joe is movin' slow

Harking back to a quieter time amid
'60s unrest and demonstration,
I remember *Petticoat Junction*
for three pretty girls and their Uncle Joe.

"That's Uncle Joe, he's a-movin' kinda slow
at the Junction." And 40 years later,
I wonder if Joe is a symbol for something
deeper or maybe just an old geezer

with creaky joints. I can tell you from here,
if he's a symbol, he's not time,
which keeps moving faster
at the Junction and toward

both terminals at the end.

Near daybreak, with a nod to Frost

The oxymoron of small-press fame

I get two contributors' copies of a folio
filled with broadsides by small-press luminaries.
They're beautifully done, on heavy cardstock,
each broadside a unique design and color. Besides
some names that are familiar to many today,
there are reprints of poems by Bukowski,
Brautigan and Ferlinghetti. My poem is sandwiched
between Bukowski's and Christopher Cunningham's.

So this is fame, small-press style. Fame indeed;
the irony being that this beautiful presentation,
like so many small-press publications,
is a limited edition of 200 copies.
So maybe someday this will be a collector's item,
but right now it means that only a few hundred
people will see this work. It's the flipside
of "it's hard to be humble when you're
as great as I am"—

it's hard to be famous
when you're as obscure as I am.

Harry Calhoun

Butterfly, here and gone

for Trina

She's away on business
and fluttering all around me tonight

the butterfly softness and brief
fragility of a summer evening

lost without her, and this beer
is small consolation but it buys me

the mood of the rest of summer
spent on her return.

The night lumbers slowly by
like a moth stuck in sludge

and I can't wait to sleep and wake

one morning closer to her

The promise, 100 percent and what clings

You ask me to change and I promise
to try, but that is not enough, you want
me to promise to succeed, something
I have done well enough for most of my life,

but none of this is 100 percent.
Nothing so prosaic or broadbrush
as the leopard changing its spots,
more like the bramble bushes of my youth.

Running through the summer field
down to Snaky Bend, the swimming hole
with my friends, the burrs sticking
to our shorts and our shirts and our legs.

And we'd pluck them off one by one
but sometimes some of them clung
until morning and we'd wake up
with our little unwanted passengers.

So I'm no stranger to waking up
with the unwanted. I'll get rid
of what I can, but some of this baggage,
some of these burrs, are in places

I don't even know exist.

The house, secure, tonight, tomorrow

Tonight and every night, teak-sided doors
the rufous-sided towhee of paneling,
the brown heavy dark but comforting
as the brown fresh birds of spring. Closure
for the bedroom, the certificate to the kitchen.

While on the other side, pristine white
faces into the modest bath.

The doors clasp us in appropriate colors,
I open them and walk past both sides
as the brown coffee perks and the aroma rises
pungent, loud and perfect

against the white noise of morning

Near daybreak, with a nod to Frost

Elsewhere than paradise

This is of traveling so I can walk
beside the sea oats by the shore
where I will hear two days from now

the shore changing, the sand shifting
I write it now but will hear it then,
that strange eternal roar

and just over the top of an eroded Appalachian
of dune is two days' expectations fulfilled,
each time I visit, the borrowed tomorrows

paid back to me, and I breathe free
and inhale salt air and exhale
the short breaths I've wasted on

making what someone calls a living
elsewhere than paradise

Harry Calhoun

My wife reading her book
in the bed beside me has no idea
of the atomic bomb about to explode

right next to her. It's just a poem
about to split itself into a profound metaphor
and a prosaic presentation

and blow someone's world apart.
At least that's what I hope. It's
all just a test, thoughts I've never had before,

not on the grand scale of Einstein
and relativity or scientists splitting the atom.
But a small sudden cataclysm of life and death,

blasting life to pieces like clay pigeons
and reassembling it all while we lie
calmly in our beds, waiting for something

to come and blow us away,
unpredictable as the next minute,

sure as tomorrow morning.

Surcease, coming

Near daybreak, with a nod to Frost

The dog is a big black shadow
with me everywhere
I go tonight

my heart is with you,
your absence the shadow
of evening, dropping without you

a few more evenings
and the black dog
will walk with us

in the shadows
that as we walk together become
invisible

Susan Alexander, the snow, 1981

Dark hair framing an alabaster face,
eyes brown almonds under long lashes,
that face I can't forget, you waiting
to deliver drinks, your subsistence to fund

your full-time job as goddess.
Marty and I off-duty bartenders
sipping away our sorrows by your station.
Marty moved on, restless as most of us

were in those days, looking for something more.
It started snowing and with business slow
the bar closed down early. You complimented
my white sweater and said I looked handsome

and asked if I'd walk you home. And
in the universe of snow swirling around us,
stars of it settling in your hair, I never settled
as close in orbit as an arm around you.

We were going home, holidays, and we smiled
and I'm sure you know I almost kissed you
as I squeezed your hand goodnight
and I think you wanted me to, but

I walked away still smiling, the wistful shuffle
of a missed opportunity
as the snow started sticking
to the ground, painting possibility,

a landscape I dreamed about that night
as flakes fell
outside my dreams
and today and many dreams

since

Near daybreak, with a nod to Frost

Dog star, protector

Crystal-clear stars, crescent moon
emerging from its melon-half self.
You think you see a ghost
beyond the deck in your back yard,
but your black dog, with you,
would be afraid if you had need to be.

Go inside, go back to sleep,
the skies are clear, the night
is perfect for dreaming

Just before the sound of one hand slapping

She complains of her attraction
to bad boys, gay men and others
she should not or cannot have.

She has a self-aware and self-
absorbed notion of her plight.
"They are the flame," she says,

"and I am the moth."
I motion to her and say,
"Come on over here and

eat my clothes."

If I had a gun

Near daybreak, with a nod to Frost

I love her and she is beside me
and I am reading a book of excellent poetry.
My dog sniffles happily on his own bed

next to ours. If I had a gun I might still
kill myself, seized with needless depression.
But I have a drink instead. So much sadness

in the world but there is always another drink
and the fully loaded gun
of tomorrow

HARRY CALHOUN

Jack o' Lantern

My wife drives away for five business days
and with every mile my smile crinkles
into a hole in my face, an old man's grimace,
a pumpkin carved into something
with a countenance it never wanted,
never asked for. I turn into something
sad and scary, my expression

carved by her absence

The last touch of my father's hand

He was frail and small, almost as if trying
to return to infancy, except I sensed
that he had ceased to try. "Goodnight, son,"
he said, and his hand in mine was as light
and trembling as a fall leaf about to fall,
as slight and trembling as I imagined
my unremembered birth, as hesitant
as the uncertainties of what comes and goes
in this world. As suddenly familiar
and alien as the first barefoot step
on fresh spring grass, as new slight and remarkable
as the first touch of loss. As if unsure of his next step.

I will live with this throughout my forever.
I hope that I can pass on the tiny contact
and the enormous impact.
Ashes and dust. Nowhere in there is touch.
I cannot tell him now, what matters, the journey

  marked in milestones of touch

The poetry game

Suddenly, like a dog bounding
over the top of the Antarctic permafrost,
the email pops up and somebody acknowledges

that you exist, need rescue. Of course
this calls for a brandy, and if the Saint Bernard
doesn't have it I'm sure you do.

It's been months out here with scarce provisions,
little acceptance and no sign of life.
Get yourself back to the computer,

warm soup and lots of liquids
and keep writing the first thing
that pops into your head. Then

drop it into Antarctica and
wait for some icy

echo

Acknowledgments

Some of the poems in this book have been published previously: "Rain, the smile, lightning, thunder" and "Near daybreak, with a nod to Frost" in *Chiron Review*, "I forgot to make her happy" in *tinfoildresses*, "If I had a gun" in *Park Bench Massacre*, "The oxymoron of small-press fame" and "The poetry game" in *Poiesis Review*, "Johannesburg" in *Orange Room Review*, "Stubble" in *Citron Review*, and "Butterfly, here and gone" in *shady side review*.

Dedication

For Trina Allen, Alex, Hillary Hebert, and Anne and Daryl Woodman for their support.

And to all those editors who saw the body of my work, warts and sweetness, and embraced it and looked on it with that same ol' decent lazy eye.

Retro

Harry Calhoun

Introduction by the Author

These are mostly poems that I wrote in the late '80s or '90s that I am still at peace with. I could certainly come up with a collection of clinkers that I might have called *Rut-roh* instead of *Retro*, but I think this represents my earlier work pretty well. I hope you enjoy.

To Trina and to a lot of good memories—
and bad memories, also known as lessons.

The cover photograph [of the chapbook] was used for the cover of my first printed chapbook, *Coming to Light*, on Abbey Cheapochapbooks, 1985.

Acknowledgments

Some of these poems have been previously published: "Allegory: The Old Minstrel and Passion" and "Railroad Werewolf" in *Third Lung Review*, "Watering Hole" in *Third Lung Review* and in the chapbook *Watering Hole*, "Aging" in the chapbook *Watering Hole*, "Baseball in October," "Pleasant Valley Before a Winter Storm," and "Evening Rainstorm Over Still Life" in *Attic in Abbey*, "Flying Dutchman in a Bottle" in the Lilliput Review broadside *Hard Transparencies*, "In the Hallway Outside the Dean's Office at the College of Fine Arts" in *Bogg*, "Hand" in the Chance Press anthology *A Common Thread*, "Zen" in *Neonbeam*, "Long Nights of Sleep" in *Synaesthesia*, "One for Hank Williams" in *Hobo Camp Review*, and "Retro" in *Kerouac's Dog*.

RETRO

The moon is full.
I love nothing
and it returns the favor.

TV has 99 channels
and the best stars
a gecko in a commercial

who could've crawled
out of my 1949-vintage
encyclopedia.

My wife is separated, beautiful
and asleep somewhere. The weather-
girl is pretty but unreachable.

•

Darkness, the radio. My best friend
said classical music
was for lonely people.

I am wondrous lonely,
driven by solitude
to the poems, the books, the window,

where the passing cloud
calves an overfull moon,
whose description we might capture,

in whose shadow we might create
meaning, profundity, romance,
in whose shadow one might create

the evening of
May 22nd.

Retro

You remember writing your way through
even though you didn't know what
you were saying or doing. It's a lot like life, as they say,
no instruction manual comes with the package.

You listened to what you heard
and wrote it down and edited it until it suited you.
You wrote in Courier New and progressed
to Times New Roman and finally settled

on Helvetica, no Arial. People told you
that non-serif fonts are easier to read,
and looking at them now, by God, you believe it.
But you'll believe anything and you think

sometimes you'll believe everything.
You believed in two marriages and countless
relationships before something real happened.
You stopped writing poems for years

and sold yourself as a marketing writer.
And you did it well, but you forgot to sell
what mattered most: what mattered to you.
And now that you're putting your self

up for sale again, look back in that old dusty mirror
and you'll see that even in the doldrums of selling out
your voice screamed through, sometimes,
like some alien bird flinging its egg tooth

at the imprisoning shell. It's an old story,
but you hope that somebody
might buy it, if only because

it is true.

(And by the way,
this is set in Times New Roman
because you're always
only halfway there.)

Watering Hole

I

The fawns congregate without drinking.
There is so little to want.
Spots waver in frog ripples
like the intercosmic
milk of stars above, and the tiny
lunk of the dive says life.
The doe is proud and silent.

All animals, all heathens
and believers know God
when quiet settles awhile.
Then the buck explodes
over the brushpile and a haiku
invades the huge
horizon of moon. Ripples sink,
molecules still. Lives rise
and set here
without cubicles or bricks.
We forget the autonomy of fur.

II

I have been the furred observer,
icelets bristling in stiff hairs
beneath the winter moon.
I am sure of it, a conscience
wild enough to say kill, feed, sleep,
mate, raise young without regret
without fear of the hatchet
hands of clock, without palms
with dominant lifelines
imprinting my infant's skull.

I know the striving toward nothing,
the freedom that grows
a millennium of skins against cold.
It is dear, but the mind is split.
I nuzzle my young in my sleep,
then grasp at a wool blanket.

III

Eight hours away now,
the work we wear like a skin,
the artificial busy-ness we inhabit
like a house. I imagine it tensed
by my desk, waiting for something
to die inside me.

But tonight the wine tells me
tales of her grape heritage.
The cello's horsehair and wood
split into forests and mustang herds
while Beethoven works his warnings.

Here, work is the leopard.
I wear its rosettes like stigmata,
but they have always washed off
in the act of creating

    from the silence the buck
    bursts from the brushpile

Harry Calhoun

thanks to Neil Young's "Pocahontas,"
for inspiration

the plane's props rock over my little box
at the top of the stairs
you have to hear this wind to understand

how the engines' drone sounds
in this April Key West breeze
and they won't let jets land here

quaint, these Keys,
the romance of the wing
propping this idyllic life alive

•

sleeping early tonight
with props above sounding foreign, oriental
turning air like swinging scimitars

i hear the wood and wind contact
of the earliest biplanes
hear the sea and sand and seaweed rush
of primeval shore

wing   carry me not out of here
only above what troubles me

•

from my second-floor porch
the silver tin roofs, the silver-
green palms breezing, and the plane

rotoring its anachronistic karma onto my island

i puzzle my place
in this tiny universe segment.
inside, The Weather Channel says:

"Vorticity is the measure
of the spin
in a small portion of the atmosphere"

i lay down think propellers   think silver
think   my wing planes
solid

in this small portion
of the atmosphere

vorticity

this poem
is measuring my spin

Harry Calhoun

Baseball in October

It's like soup, cooked with love. It seems a sin.
The time, the luxurious ingredients.
Ah, but the aroma. The slow simmer,

now it's done, a summer broiling. Baseball late,
this travesty, the gesture out of season; tweed
in July, tanktop in October. But look: the catcher's mitt,

cool leathery stomach waiting for the mulligatawny
of the knuckler, dropping like a leaf
in the unpredictable breeze.

We plop our savor and spirit
secure and warm by the TV, outside
the days chilled as if fanned by bat's swipe.

Sand below, memories of beaches,
the plate the eternal measure. Past summer,
the poetry of a good changeup.

The eyes, the mitts, the bats are all waiting
Tureens, ladles of midsummer hail,
the temperature now.

Baseball. Cool nights I still want to stroll
down to Woolworth's for shoelaces and sodas.
The TV, the heroes, it makes me remember.

That's the best part.
The chill, the brace, holds up my boyish back,
it makes me remember.

RETRO

Pleasant Valley Before a Storm

Here near valley-bottom the beeches and maples
among the hillside's rolling purplish browns
see the first gray hairs on a great head.
The roil above, pewter-silver, tarnish and shine,
the buff and polish of slow and rapid change.
When my gaze snaps from skyward, I feel I fall
from unity as a spark from flux. My feet
crush motionless grasses, cold-tanned, trampled
already by now-melted early snows.
There is a tree my father cut to firewood
stacked by the gray garage, lying full
of termites' cellular paths. Nothing moves there,
now; I look and turn away.

In midfield there is a log rotting, damp
as a spent lover, one with the sodden earth.
A perfection passion craves.

My sentience crawls over all, quick as a bug
and as mindless. Trying to assemble the sinking
to dampened dust that already makes too much sense.
The hills close in pushed by the steely rush of sky;
chimneys shoo away warm ghosts of flame. I mosey inside,
perversely savoring the insistent nip that bids me linger,
shivering in my cozy wool jacket.
I have a longing for logs afire, the two clear reds
of fireplace and claret and a doze on the couch.
I waken near morning, rise to touch the windowpane,
tangible, cold. Snow covers the log, falls in the field;
the ground will freeze, spurning the gentle meld of the wood.

From my mindless appreciation protrudes
a nagging jut of thought, for that part of field
once tree, fertility lying dormant

beneath a cool, quick, beautiful veneer.

Evening Rainstorm Over Still-Life in Attic

Violinists lean to their strings
and their melodies oil my stereo.
In the rain, in the dark-coming-down,
despite the fog the city has lit
votive candles for you here at dusk.
The buildings lift lit necklaces, jewels,
rain plops like plump truffles
into this evening soup.
The atmosphere is set;
all breaths wait for you.

Through the window the roofs
seem to buckle under torrents and ripple,
crazy, bats' wings. I break from the clear
pane bludgeoned obscure, portraiture painted—
we could spend our lives watching—
and go sit, sipping brandy in the dark.
I will let memories rain in but will not sniff
their mildewed aromas. I will hold them
like a cobbler baked in an airtight oven.
I will not look out the window.

In the morning maybe things will clear.

In the Hallway Outside the Dean's Office at the College of Fine Arts

There's a statue of Diana,
the goddess of the hunt.
When I peek beneath
her marble skirt,
I see she has no

real existence
because her legs are sculpted together
at the upper thigh.
No human could live
like that! I point this out

to a guy in the office
but he doesn't care
about art. He likes politics.
He shows me a photo
of Reagan giving a speech

under a bust of Lenin.
I tell him I'd rather see
the bust of the blond
secretary down the hall.
I'm kidding, I prefer brunettes,

but I wonder
why humor and art
so often emerge
from the clothes
we hide them under.

One for Hart Crane

Heard you jumped overboard.
How was the water?
Damn, lousy fishing weather

for poets that day. You sunk
good, found your niche. Drowning.
Finally, something you did as well

as writing.

•

Homosexual, drunken, brilliant,
before the sun rose on Capote.
Spaniards drowned their horses

to lighten their ships
in these latitudes. Centuries later,
you jettisoned, spare cargo.

You saved Everybody
a problem. And hell, even your poems
had no elsewhere to swim.

•

So how are those scattered bones?
I won't make you talk;
my voice hears yours fine.

You can trust me. I can't swim
either. So the world was your oyster,
and you didn't like oysters.

You had to see if water
turned to wine at rock bottom.
If you could have something to drink

with whatever you could stomach.

●

I can't make it different.
But I understand how hard it was.
You'd shrug if you had shoulder.

You did what I haven't.
I'm doing what you can't.
Night deepens. I grow colder.

"Hi, thanks for thinking. One thing:
'Goodbye, everybody.' Guess
acceptable was my dress

'til the final breath. Too much
a poet to hurl
my copulatory epithets

at the world."

●

Poetry, the pearl we form
around the pain. Dive deep
enough and find this one,

Crane, still mired in murk,
but finally
going with the flow.

Flying Dutchman in a Bottle

Frame of reference: For the duration of this poem,
I give my world clear boundaries,
imagine it a bottle. I give my fear
soul and vehicle, suppose it
a three-masted schooner lashed
by torrents, tempest-tossed.

Loneliness needs no imagination;
I have been confined in self
since washing ashore from the womb,
the part I call soul
a bird too long aloft,
bumping headlong into body
on its way to desperate rest.

•

I do not really believe this.
I have no faith in the preposterous;
I am unsuited for life. I believe
for the poem's duration, believe because
creativity keeps me moving, moving
so that evil's tiny grit
grows no pearl in me. It is a game,
the poem's religion keeping me
thinking within boundaries of lines,
lines that may lead beyond
this metaphorical bottleneck.

Serious frivolity, figuring a poem's puzzle;
explaining in ways that resolve nothing
or help us face nothing. I can fabricate
for myself
how the ship got in the bottle,
fit down the bottleneck,
how all that alters us happens.

The birth of legend, in microcosm,
may be a need for explanations
where imaginations touch reality.

•

Imagine, we are angels turned cynical,
aging. Angels got *us* for bodies.

Bodies, our pelts
against the shiver of existence:
Shiver that comes in a mist,
in stormy seas, on turbulent waves,
in the time when panic grips the guide wheel,
the specter that throws the final chill
up the back of a torrent-soaked mac.

When the bad omen hazes over us,
under us like the arch of bottle
and we know

nothing breaks in from outside,
nothing busts the clear shell,
we are trapped
and it doesn't matter
if the ship

is just a trick of the mist.

Groceries

Fresh produce is healthy,
but bulky, so we lugged it
together. Having steered me

from processed cheese and pizza,
she helped me carry, climb three stairflights
through firedoors to our flat.

Then she said going out the door
was healthier for her
than struggling to ask admittance.

Even downstairs, I couldn't haul
what's left of her
in a thousand breathless trips.

•

I never unlearn the expectation.
I sigh at the top of the stairs,
the effort this has become.

I have to lay something down.
One step at a time. The key unlocks
where I stay. As the door yawns quietly,

I sleepwalk back for the bags.
It's silent, as if I were deaf.
I can be dumb or talk-to-myself crazy.

Even home, I have my hands full.
I walk in alone, I think of the phrase
"beside myself," and I know

what they mean.

Allegory: The Old Minstrel and Passion

and this scar he says the big one
leaped like flame and burned in
years ringing memory

like days ago
when I grew too close
to a girl who'd grown

no bell in her soul
for me

it had nothing to do with age,
her lack; the clapper and dome
grow in some for one other

as a shell
around a pearl
around a sand grain.

There peals probably a bell
for her now in a different forest,
no music for my ears;

no alarum or clanging,
no upset for me, just
the ache and dream one feels

drinking in the mournful buoy-bell
by the quay, mist
softening and dampening down

an inexhaustible flame

Courage

Another loss. A late attack that caught me
with my roots still a little loose, and any afterblast
might serve to topple.

A Christian friend tries to comfort.
"God is crying," she says. "God is sad, and God
is angry at her for breaking the promise."

My Zen leanings kick in. Poor God, anthropomorphic enough
already, a car-driving dog or talking whale
saddled with our faults. But I try to imagine

God, which I fancy as *That Which Comes To Me
When I Write*, or *That Which Makes Everything Go
Somewhat OK, Usually*

as crying, angry, and sad. God sounds
a lot like me, right now. I snuggle up
to the concept like a kitten.

•

All right. It hurts. Over the years I've learned
all the tricks, getting over the series of surprises
called my life. Write through it,

keep moving, see the women, read more,
do bars and movies and all the dodges.
I've learned them all but courage.

Me, who boyish read of the RAF commandos
seat-of-the-pants fighting enemies in the forest.
This long. Still in the woods. But I'll find it.

I can always get through. But like God, I'm sad,
I suffer. This time will be different.
This time I will wring these tears out

in my fists, crush them until they give up
the secret. Suffering only bruises us
when we wriggle too hard

against it.

Railroad Werewolf

I have been traveling this rail since I conceived it.
For the few blessed or cursed, words carry the taint.

So the journey mutates. The sport in the blood
and the word are the tide and moon lovemaking,

not the separation most of the world endures.
Early I was thrown from the track and savaged

by a lust for a gentle art. My birthright only a growl,
a hunger, I began stalking my children.

For them I will suffer anything. This curse,
watching the windows like frames, my life. The movie

is boring. Scenery is scenery. It goes on forever
and ultimately is finite. But if I ravage it correctly,

the blood will change with my taint. The scenery
slaughtered cold will live forever.

•

I have watched the moon grow barren
and ovulate. And in its pregnancy, swollen,

the ripe savagery of ideas; Artemis the stag
sought for seduction by slow wolves.

I have kept my composure,
stayed the fang,

felt the sway of water
tugging the follicles until testosterone

shimmered through my hair.
Holding my teeth to a snarl

till morning's coherence gave them meat.

•

I am tired, waking to an empty car
once filled with hobos.

They drink their every days straight.
They reach the excess that kills them,

then they want more. I cannot be filled with their food,
drunk on their liquor. So I sit with it, sleep with it,

starving and sober, until I change.

I am the legend that has no friends,
incisor that poisons others

with its disease.

•

Waking solitary, tired, devoid
of the transients, the steady clack of the rails,

the dull green, the cows out the windows
seem tolerable. What made me bend

life's track this way will change no one
here last night. It's just me, the empty car,

and the savage urge I will post at the next depot.
But the stragglers will be back. Meanwhile, doomed,

I am proud to be whistlestopping
toward the silver bullet with my name.

Whatever venom lasts from my bite,
whatever howl the train trails,

my gypsy legacy
is marrow in the bone:

The way you walk is thorny,
through no fault of your own.

Fog, trees to grasp, the journey,
a chance at changing the temporary

is what I own.

Poetry as a Dying Medium

> "Is poetry a dying medium?"
> —interview question to this poet

Hold hands around the table.
Poetry, the medium who pulled voices from the ectoplasm,
who made the planchette squeak and shake
for the Ouija's response, who caused Clara Smith
to cry by arranging a visitation
from her late beloved Jake,

is dying. Her tricks go with her
to the grave. Smooth charlatan, manipulating words
and events, showing what is beyond by describing
what is not. On her deathbed the medium
begins to believe in herself, a Christ of poems,
sees that beneath the trickery is a vehicle

after all, a light on the other side.
She stretches her left hand wide to be led.
Her right is clenched in a fist. When the left hand
clasps around something unseen, she remains there,
forever. A light rises above her, hovers.

Perhaps there is something to this after all.
The room fills with mourners. People need to cry,
to laugh, to be reassured by whatever device
their passions live on somewhere: Poetry takes them
beyond, to deathbed dignity, a world without subterfuge,
makes dying seem as clean and holy

as the day they were born.

HARRY CALHOUN

This Light, That Portraiture

We sit till the light on the mirror,
bent by time, resembles our face.
Or someone's; we will settle
for grubbing the pocketbook bottom
when we have lost something.

We want to paint *now*
but we have lost our signature.
So now sits naked before us
as we fumble for car keys.
We want to show our etchings

but they're blank. The acid
can't autograph the surface,
as if it's moving too fast.

•

Light floods the study.
It's a grand ballroom, studded
with portraits of the magnificent dead.
When life called, we followed.
Never occurred to us

that it wanted to dance.
So down the neck into the bottle
we filed, and from a full ship
looked out on this light,
that portraiture

waltzing,
assembling
before us.

•

The sun on our backs
sends metaphors, warmth
and shadow. Art tells you only
what you feel. We spend sun cycles
learning the tricks

of the trade. Burned by exposure,
the light only heat,
seeing the portrait's illusion
in an empty mirror:
The image of a shaking head.

It's all trade.
There are no
tricks.

Sleeping Beauty

You know, sometimes I think
that somewhere inside you
there's a you that loves me.

She's sleeping and waiting
for the right time to wake up.
And someday, some nature, some sun

in its sudden shine, some alarm
will wake you. And you'll realize
that love, rise joyous

and walk down the stairs.
And I'll be there, smiling,
having my coffee,

tired but happy,
having been awake

for such a long, long time.

Aging

The bones stand staunch
against the fear wiggling
in my brain. Holding
my mother's letter, remembering
the neat, looped words.
And now, the shake and jerk
of arthritic scrawl
like New Year's confetti
let loose and trampled
on the sheet.

Nothing gets better forever.
Champagne goes sour,
beer flattens out,
and the kiss's lips
are pulled back in death.
With my grandmother's passing
there are no more grandparents
on either side of the family.
My folks can see their way
clear now.

Would the friends of my youth understand
if I called them here together
and asked them
to look again at
the hands they thought
held all the cards
on the table now? Quick
before the creases grow deeper,
ruts in the pocked roads
on the palms we once
thought held our fortune,

  hands the means to our maps.

Harry Calhoun

Zen

My lover, so much better at the Zen path I admire,
is leaving. I can't pursue that road because

who can pursue a road—how Zen—
and because pursuit catches the wrong beast's tail.

And there is no beast.

Tonight I come from my walk as rain falls.
Partially packed, she sits serenely on the couch.
I puff in and take off my clothes. Then redress.

I want to go back out and sit in the rain.
This urge is because the air,
when the rain began,

smelled like laundry mixed with hot biscuits.
I need to re-experience that. And I need to ponder
now.   I bring a beer.   It suspends Western disbelief;

we need training wheels, sometimes.
This bench seems carved of the stone
of Japanese lanterns. I sit till I'm drenched.

Soon the rain slackens.
I'm treated to an accidental duet
of treefrog and evening bird.

Fireflies rise in the mist
like steam from biscuits, laundry.
I am fine until I come back in

and she is there.
Life is suffering, sure. But why cool,
drenched with Zen,

I feel it, and she lives through it?
The answer, I intuit, is in the accidental duet of treefrog

and evening bird, while fireflies rise steamlike,
incredibly sad, pretty, but just

doing what they do.

HARRY CALHOUN

Infection

> "The Hawk's Song":
> The ancient Egyptians believed that,
> when someone died,
> the soul flew off to the West as a hawk.

Instinct told me to gorge:
Something much smaller than me
but oh so many more
an insectivorous blanket

wiggling, niggling, insinuating
around me as I flew.
I, the fast hawk, mind you,
slaying diver flashing falcon charm,
power like sex from swift talons.

Now something small, swallowed
has laid eggs in my soft belly
during a moment's dart
through the swarm, now dreaming
I vision me carrion, eaten from within,
slowed and opened as a broken
cantaloupe on the plain. Oh the slow

buzzards will have me, finally,
turkey-necks savoring the feast
these maggots have made me.
I tell you, time catches up.
I preen feathers, try to cover
moving holes in my body.

Goddamn, they never tell you.
You fly so fast,
not to let it catch you, then

a twinge, spasm, the little build
of pain

you fly so fast
not to let it catch you
you slow down
and surprise

in the very beak that's fed you
you catch *it*.

One for Hank Williams

The train moans here around daybreak.
I have a fantasy I use
to ride the rail back to sleep:

I'm lost and alone and it's cold
but I've found some shelter and covers
and drift as the snow falls to sleep

and that scenario
(train echoes o-o-o)
carries me usually back

but this morning I lay tossing
as if strapped to the tracks
thinking of Luke the Drifter.

•

This dawn, the pigeons' coos could sing backup
for that lonesome whippoorwill
and the train whistle sounds oddly off-key

always, a note of leaving and longing.
This is not for the fat and comfortable.
This is about losing the will to live.

This is for simple intelligence
strapped to a heart so big
you just knew it'd burst. Strapped

sticky as blackstrap
to a rail clacking 29-29-29-29.
And sometimes at dinners

when boxcars of small talk blur by
I raise a silent glass
and make a connection

back to a depot, a dusty boyhood
before I understood
that the incomprehensible

jambalaya crawfish pie filé gumbo lingo
was just restless words
to fill in the time.

I felt the shot-down hero
leaving the country bar
with nothing but a cheap cigar

and underneath the "Hey Good Lookin'" bravado
I sensed what Hank was saying:
"I'm so lonesome

I could cry."

HARRY CALHOUN

Long Nights of Sleep

in memory of the near stroke of 8/8/82,
for Robert Gregory

I

Liquor delays the inevitability
of confinement, postpones the mind
dragging to work, the words
clicking in chained lines
inhabiting the cells of paper. Days
have stretched into years, miming
bourbon's tired elastic that yo-yos
idly talking minutes into weeks,
weeks, weeks into the rest
of your life, life. Down a long bar
eight years built on minutes ago,
my body said no to the comparative
seconds of sleep, the doubles of bourbon,
the anxiety for the duet
I no longer helped comprise
washing its hands
and feasting its eyes
on Minneapolis.

II

Clinically speaking:
Blood clot leaves shaky moorings, travels
upvein, settles in retina, blows up
half the left side like the leaf-bomber
sweeping in autumn. And you rest,
rest, sleep comes with the authority
of a lesson, rest, and a drink or two
and the corpse in you
crawls out, the opened rose
of a book you're too beat to read
falls on your chest.

I slept in a state of grace.
I only wakened for spare moments,
thirsting for cool, dry deserts of sheets
and pillow-dunes, feeling
the drench of night air
in my third-floor oasis. Then
the profound tiredness would call
me back to rest.

III

Mornings I'd drag
from my cover-cocoon
still tired,
odd in the world
as a moth just emerged.
Flutter to my desk lamp,
to the bright lair
of the monster Creativity.
Leading the beast
by that candle-hand of light,
daring it to use a few
of its 150 fingers of IQ
to pull some petals
off a flowering thought.

But Creativity was deaf and half-blind.
I slept my deathlike sleeps for a year,
dreams of moths ricocheting,
crocheting the lacy-shadowed
night, monsters lurking
in every small but dark
and anxious waking moment.

IV

I sit now in this tenth year
of my afterlife, humming with energy
and enjoying the dawn
of this blessed insomnia,
sipping a beer
and struggling to jot my thoughts.

These litanies I write have become
my prayers, against that death
that came to pin me down in sleep
but wasn't quite big enough.
Have become my warning, that weakness
is the strongest force there is.
The brittle skeleton endures
when the flesh is trash.

The sun will come up soon
and it looks like I will be with it.
I have been allowed to live
and have learned a few things
along the way. Why, just now,
in this book I've been reading,
my eyes fall on a mid-page sentence:

*Most plants will not flower
until the day reaches a certain length.*

The universe, Calhoun,
the very universe
draws things
from long nights of sleep.

RETRO

Hand

I am the hand waving goodbye
severed because I could not
keep its gentle pressure
at your back
to urge the dance I wanted

I am the hand waving bravely
don't see me if you don't love me
my voice wavering like your resolution

but you left
on a handshake

•

I have the magical poem I wrote
about a field full of fireflies

you have the hand waving byebye
fluttering by like a butterfly

both graze our eyelids
batlike at odd moments

of sleep

waking

and that in-between nostalgia

that shaking hand

remorse

For Jennifer

once upon a 4 a.m. outside the
Appelrouth Grille in Key West ...

I had just been manhandled
(woman with no patience no heart)
and my friend you came staggering

pretty long-limbed and blasted
into the china shop of my life
no bull   gazelle-like

and we outside on the bench
bar-after by the Appelrouth
the stars just the distance I needed

I thought I glimpsed beauty again

you said:

I could go to sleep
if I had something soft
for my head

I offered a manger of bony shoulder
it must've been good enough
out like a light

I looked over, up
the close-eyed blond-framed life mask
this platinum moon
all its faces turning full

you could launch
the ships to Troy anew
beauty full aflame in your innocence

and for me
kittens played harpsichords
my grandma was alive and baking
cinnamon rolls   all the playful sex
and first kisses   magic
is the best reality

in my dream you never woke
we stayed
the moon drifting mid-phase always

in my dream
that would become this poem

Waiting for the Newspaper

Too dark and early for even the keyhole,
the newspaper begs me open the door.
Brusquely breaking my bliss like a cracked bat,
on a sweet spot of hardwood
the splat of our transience
stamped on trees.

Before this we listened to birds' trilling;
before this we wound ourselves as a timepiece
of hazy morning thoughts. We greened
in the nothing shoots sprout from. We bend
to pick up. Now curiosity gets the best of us.
After it gets the best, what's left?

We should apologize for opening the door.
Survey the newsprint, the grain of the floor.
Wood. The differences. Out the window,
maples, red with fire. Close the door.
Apologize for leaving that outside,
for bringing this in.

Leaving

It's like a door closing.
I want it to be gentle, noiseless,

Japanese. Reopen it and apologize
to the wood if it slams.

But humidity swells this
beyond what it should be

and the squeak and push
to close it sounds

as if I beg
to be let back in.

Harry Calhoun and his dog, Alex, in 2009.

Harry Calhoun at his typewriter, 1985.

Colophon

The edition you are holding is the First Print Edition of this complete anthology publication. It comprises five previous individual chapbooks originally published without ISBNs, spanning from 1993 to 2012, with single outtake pieces from various other projects spanning from 2003 to 2014. The included chapbooks, now in paperback for the first time, are: *Just Because I Didn't Leave the Driving to Us I Got Jailed and Juiced Good* by Paul Weinman (first reprinted July 1993), *The History of Candles* by Joseph Verrilli (January 2003), *Body English* by Joseph Verrilli (March 2009), *Near daybreak, with a nod to Frost* by Harry Calhoun (May 2010), and *Retro* by Harry Calhoun (April 2012).

The cover title font and interior titles are set in Aniyah, created by Din Studio, used with a full commercial license. The alternative non-serif cover font, headers, footers, and captions are set in Avenir Book, created by Adrian Frutiger. The back cover Alternating Current Press logo font is set in Portmanteau, created by JLH Fonts. All other fonts are set in Marion, created by Ray Larabie, except for the poem "Retro," which is set in Times New Roman. All fonts are used with permission; all rights reserved.

The front cover was designed by Leah Angstman using the artwork "A Perch of Birds" by Hector Giacomelli, 1880. The Alternating Current lightbulb logo was created by Leah Angstman, ©2006, 2020 Alternating Current. The Violet Ray logo was created by Leah Angstman, ©2020 Alternating Current. The cover for *Just Because I Didn't Leave the Driving to Us I Got Jailed and Juiced Good* was created by Suburban Wilderness Press. The cover for *The History of Candles* was drawn by Leah Angstman. The cover for *Body English* was designed by Leah Angstman using a photograph supplied by Joseph Verrilli. All nature photographs in Harry Calhoun's chapbooks were taken by T. Kilgore Splake, with covers designed by Leah Angstman. The photographs of Paul Weinman, Joseph Verrilli, and Harry Calhoun were supplied by the authors. The 2009 photo of Harry Calhoun was taken by John Pagliuca. All images are used with permission; all rights reserved.

The editors wish to thank the font and graphic creators for allowing legal use of their work.

OTHER WORKS FROM
Alternating Current Press

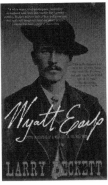

All of these books (and more) are available at
Alternating Current's website: press.alternatingcurrentarts.com.

alternatingcurrentarts.com

Made in the USA
Columbia, SC
24 October 2020